T0088218

Your GODDESS YEAR

A WEEK-BY-WEEK GUIDE TO INVOKING THE DIVINE FEMININE

SKYE ALEXANDER

Adams Media

New York   London   Toronto   Sydney   New Delhi

Aadamsmedia

Adams Media
An Imprint of Simon & Schuster, Inc.
57 Littlefield Street
Avon, Massachusetts 02322

First Adams Media trade paperback edition December 2019

ADAMS MEDIA and colophon are trademarks of Simon & Schuster.

For information about special discounts for bulk purchases, please contact Simon & Schuster Special Sales at 1-866-506-1949 or business@simonandschuster.com.

The Simon & Schuster Speakers Bureau can bring authors to your live event. For more information or to book an event contact the Simon & Schuster Speakers Bureau at 1-866-248-3049 or visit our website at www.simonspeakers.com.

Interior design by Erin Alexander
Interior illustrations by Emma Taylor

Manufactured in China

10 9 8 7 6 5 4 3 2 1

Library of Congress Cataloging-in-Publication Data has been applied for.

ISBN 978-1-5072-1105-2
ISBN 978-1-5072-1106-9 (ebook)

DEDICATION

In memory of my sister and beautiful goddess, Myke Perkins.

CONTENTS

ACKNOWLEDGMENTS

Once again, I am indebted to the many talented people at Adams Media for making this book possible, especially my editor, Eileen Mullan. Thanks, too, to Katie Corcoran Lytle, Erin Alexander, and everyone else who helped bring my idea to fruition.

INTRODUCTION

Protection. Guidance. Power.

Our ancestors worshipped pantheons of deities that helped them interpret the universe and their place in it. These gods and goddesses—along with lesser divinities—personified the energetic forces that operated in the cosmos and governed all life on earth. The earliest deities were female creator figures such as the Babylonians' Tiamat; the Chinese goddess Xi Wangmu; and the Hopi's Spider Grandmother, who brought our planet and the heavenly bodies into being.

Later goddesses represented various aspects of the Divine Feminine, the creative power of the universe. These goddesses were earth and fertility goddesses who made the crops grow, love goddesses who guided human relationships, and protector goddesses who kept mortals safe from birth to death and beyond. The ancients saw the Goddess wherever they looked: in the sun, moon, and stars, in the rivers and mountains, in the wind and rain. She ruled everything. She *was* everything.

In this book, you'll meet fifty-two of these omnipotent goddesses—one for each week of the year—and learn about their virtues, their roles in the spiritual traditions of many cultures, and their significance and influence in our lives today. (Please note that because each deity is aligned with a seven-day period, the "months" don't necessarily begin on the first day of a month.) Many of the goddesses are introduced on the dates our ancestors honored them with festivals and other rituals, some of which people around the world continue to celebrate. The ancients ascribed earthly events such as floods, earthquakes, and volcanoes to the actions of these powerful deities; they believed they needed to appeal to and appease the goddesses with festivities in order to attract divine blessings and prevent calamities.

The Babylonians, for instance, engaged in eleven days of ceremonies at the beginning of the spring planting season to praise the fertility goddess Tiamat and solicit her aid in producing healthy crops. In India, Hindus worship the goddess Kali during the festival Kali Puja, a night when evil spirits are said to abound. The festival honors the fierce destroyer goddess and petitions her protection from these spirits.

Other goddesses are presented on dates that relate to their personal attributes and histories—or rather *herstories*. Many goddess myths emerged in early agrarian civilizations, when people lived close to the earth. Mother Earth herself is often thought of as a physical manifestation of the Divine Feminine. Therefore, this book aligns the goddesses with the times of the year that exemplify their characteristics in accordance with nature's cycles. Spring, for instance, is a time of promise and hope, when the earth reawakens after her long sleep. Youthful and beautiful goddesses, such as the Romans' Flora who governs spring flowers, represent the rejuvenation, fertility, and new beginnings we associate with this season. Winter goddesses symbolize the final stage of life. Like the Gnostics' Sophia, they appear as wise elders who encourage us to discover our inner strength and the deeper meaning of human existence.

As you work your way through the book you'll likely notice similarities in the legends and lore surrounding the various deities, although the stories also contain features distinctive to the cultures in which they arose. All civilizations have creation myths, for instance. According to Chinese legend, the mother goddess Xi Wangmu wove the universe into existence—ancient images often show her holding a loom. We find a similar story in Native American lore, which says the creator deity Spider Woman wove a great web that holds everything in the cosmos together.

Different versions of the myths exist too, for they've evolved over time and reflect sociopolitical developments, geological events, and the perspectives of the storytellers who handed them down through the ages. But no matter the similarities—and differences—among the goddesses' stories, as you read the legends about them you'll marvel at their strength in the face of adversity; their wisdom, compassion, and patience; and their insight and ingenuity.

THE POWER OF THE GODDESSES

As you work with the goddesses, you'll come to understand their relevance not only in the past but today as well. By inviting and honoring them, you have much to gain. You don't have to like or approve of a particular goddess to learn from her saga and benefit from what she teaches. Oftentimes a deity will challenge you to take a good hard look at what you value and confront parts of yourself that may not be pretty. You'll see aspects of the goddesses in yourself and recognize their trials and triumphs as things you, too, may experience. Perhaps, like Rhiannon, you feel betrayed by someone you trusted—her courage can show you how to bear the hurt and gain strength through patient perseverance. Diana can teach you the importance of independence and self-sufficiency. Brigid can spark your creativity and inspire you to express your artistic talents confidently. Each goddess offers you a gift and shares a lesson for your continued growth.

They'll also connect you with the seasons; the earth and the cosmos; and the ongoing cycle of birth, death, and rebirth. In our modern society, many of us have lost touch with nature's rhythms; as a result, we feel isolated and out of touch with the world in which we live. Working with goddess energy will help restore your connection to the Divine Feminine—the creative power of the universe—and our planet as her most fundamental symbol. In so doing, you'll learn to ride the ebbs and flows in your personal relationships, your career path, your health and well-being without losing your center. You'll come to see yourself as an integral part of the greater whole, and gain a deeper sense of belonging in this world and the world beyond.

INVITING THE GODDESSES

For each goddess, in addition to learning about her specific herstory and power, you'll find a suggested ritual, meditation, or other activity that you can use to connect with her. Some are based on traditional rites and festivities and are intended to help you draw upon goddess energy to enrich your life and to bring you into harmony with the natural cycles that still influence us even if we live in cities made of steel, glass, and concrete. Feel free to adapt these rituals to suit your individual circumstances—or to create your own from scratch.

Other practices are designed to help you use the goddesses' experiences to address certain situations or areas in your own life. For example, Inanna's act of surrendering at each of the seven gates of her sister's palace is echoed in the chakra-opening ritual suggested during the week dedicated to her.

Throughout you'll also find sidebars that offer ideas for extended study and consideration. "Symbols and Correspondences" mentions flowers, gemstones, objects, etc. associated with a particular goddess; these reveal aspects of her nature. The compassionate Asian goddess Kuan Yin, for example, holds a vial of water with which she "waters" life on earth. Once you understand the symbols and correspondences, you can incorporate them into your rituals.

"Friends and Foes" describes a goddess's allies and adversaries, deities who may assist or thwart her efforts. Familiarizing yourself with these related goddesses can provide additional insights into your own relationships and the hidden parts of yourself.

Animals and birds accompany many goddesses, and these are discussed as "Her Animal Totems." Totems, or spirit animals, serve as divine helpers, while also representing distinctive qualities associated with a particular goddess.

Sometimes you can work with a goddess more effectively by going to a place that holds her energy. Sitting beside a stream, for instance, can put you in touch with the African river goddess Oshun. "Where to Seek Her" offers suggestions for communing with the deities in this way.

Whether you're looking to connect to the Divine Feminine, honor a goddess, or receive the gift she offers, you can use the dates assigned to each goddess in this book to draw upon age-old practices and petition her assistance. Perhaps early devotees believed the goddesses' powers peaked at these times, or they felt they could communicate better with the deities on certain days of the year. Use these sacred dates to strengthen your goddess connections.

That said, when inviting the goddesses keep in mind that their placement throughout the year—whether due to festivals held in their honor or to their stories—doesn't mean you *can't* work with them at other times; invite them to join you whenever you feel a need for their presence or their power. For example, Nike, the goddess of victory, expresses qualities astrologers attribute to the zodiac sign Aries, so she's recognized in this book during the week of April 3–9. But if you're engaging in a competition in September, it's okay to call on Nike for help then too. You don't need to limit yourself to only one goddess at a time either. For example, in Greek mythology, Nike and Athena were friends, so you might want to invite both deities to assist you. Summon those whose powers seem most appropriate to your purposes.

And remember, the information shared here affords only a tiny glimpse into what these goddesses represent to the people who honor them. A vast, colorful, and inspiring body of mythology exists, and I hope you'll choose to delve into it more deeply. Now turn the page and invite the power of the goddesses into your life.

> *"There is a privacy about [winter] which no other season gives you...only in the winter, in the country, can you have longer, quiet stretches when you can savor belonging to yourself."*
>
> —Ruth Stout, American author

JANUARY

In the dark, cold, barren month of January, we plumb our inner resources, deal with winter's hardships, and hope for good things to come. January's self-reliant goddesses—Sophia, Skadi, Xi Wangmu, Athena, and Brigid—personify strength, independence, imagination, and wisdom. In this section, you'll visit with these deities. You'll hear their stories and learn to use them to engage your own inner strength. Remember, January offers a fresh start, a new year. If you've been struggling to find the impetus to change, you'll find it here.

SOPHIA

DATES FOR INVITING HER: *January 1–7*

Winter is a time of turning within, of rest, and of seeking wisdom in the dark places. As we begin the New Year, we also look forward to brighter times ahead. This week, we honor the goddess Sophia, whose name means "wisdom" in Greek, and whose divine knowledge chases away darkness and confusion, replacing them with peace.

> ### Friends and Foes
>
> Gnosticism connects Sophia with both the Virgin Mary and Mary Magdalene. We also see parallels between Sophia and goddesses in many myths and cultures, including Athena (January 22–28), Kuan Yin (March 5–11), Shakti, and Tara (June 12–18).

HERSTORY

One of the most beloved goddesses, Sophia personifies the feminine creative force in the universe. She's revered in many spiritual and religious traditions. Some Judeo-Christian sources describe her as the wisdom of God or as God's female soul. The Gnostics (a term that derives from the Greek word for "knowledge") considered her an actualization of Divine

Wisdom, wisdom incarnate. The Eastern Orthodox Church, in particular, honors her as a high-ranking divinity—her magnificent church in Istanbul, Hagia Sophia, is one of the Seven Wonders of the World.

Mythology tells us Sophia longed to share her vast knowledge with humankind to alleviate suffering on earth, apparently in the belief that knowledge and truth will set you free. Indeed, some took her up on her offer, including the great King Solomon (who's known for being wise).

According to a Gnostic story, Sophia lived in the realm of perfect light—the light of Source and Divine Wisdom. One day she descended from this exalted realm, tricked by forces from the underworld who ensnared and raped her. She gave birth to demigods known as the archons, including the Demiurge, who imbued earth with all its ills and failings. The compassionate goddess rued the damage done by her son, and, when she eventually escaped the darkness on earth to return to her celestial home, she left part of her light behind to counter evil with love.

REASONS TO INVITE HER

If you're struggling with a murky situation and need clarity to understand what's going on and how to deal with it, ask Sophia to shine her light on the matter so you can separate truth from delusion. If you're going through a dark period, this beautiful goddess can illuminate your path and guide you to a brighter, happier place. Sophia shows you what Swiss psychiatrist C.G. Jung called the "Shadow," the hidden, unacknowledged part of yourself, and she teaches you to love your dark side. Not only does she bring self-realization; Sophia can assist you in your quest for knowledge of any kind.

Her Animal Totems

Sophia is often shown with a dove, a symbol of peace, as her companion. A biblical story says Sophia assumed the form of a dove to visit the Virgin Mary when she learned she would become pregnant with Jesus.

HOW TO INVITE HER

Perform this ritual at night, in a darkened room, to elicit wisdom and insight from Sophia. Writing in a journal allows you to clarify your intention and to record your thoughts and impressions for future reference. You'll need:

- *A journal, notebook, or piece of paper*
- *A pen or pencil*
- *12 white votive candles, one for each month of the coming year*
- *12 ceramic coasters or ashtrays (optional)*
- *A cushion, pillow, or chair (optional)*
- *A black veil, headscarf, or cloth large enough to cover your head*
- *Matches or a lighter*

1. Writing in your journal or notebook with the pen or pencil, describe a subject, situation, or other matter about which you seek knowledge from the goddess.
2. Position the unlit candles on the floor, in a circle large enough that you can sit inside it. Make sure the candles can burn there safely. (You may want to set them on ceramic coasters or in ashtrays.)
3. If you've chosen to sit on a cushion, pillow, or chair, place it in the center of the circle, facing east.
4. Step inside the circle, sit, and cover your head with the veil, scarf, or cloth. This represents the veil of darkness, the shadowy quandary in which you find yourself.
5. Sit for a while, breathing slowly and deeply, while you form an image in your mind of the issue that you don't fully understand as yet.

6. When you feel ready, remove the veil.
7. Beginning in the east, move in a clockwise direction and light the candles.
8. Return to your seat and enjoy the soft candlelight illuminating the space. Listen to Sophia's voice, sharing insights and guidance with you.
9. When you feel you've received all you can for the time being, thank Sophia and extinguish the candles, moving in a counterclockwise direction.
10. In your journal, write down what Sophia has revealed to you.

SKADI

This week we honor Skadi, the Norse goddess of winter. *Scandinavia* means "Skadi's Isle." Like many other winter goddesses, Skadi is associated with darkness and death, for now the barren earth slumbers beneath a blanket of snow. Despite the bitter conditions, this goddess's strength and determination enable her to cope with challenges, as we all must do during hard times.

Her Animal Totems

Some sources suggest Skadi may have hunted with wolves, or perhaps dogs from the north country, such as Siberian huskies. Snowy owls, who symbolize wisdom as well as predatory skills, may also have accompanied her on her hunting expeditions.

HERSTORY

Folklore describes Skadi as a giantess with pale blonde hair and blue eyes who lived in Thrymheim, her father's court, high in the snow-covered mountains where winter reigned year-round. One day her father, the frost god Thiazi, decided to abduct a beautiful young goddess named Idun. For his crime, the top Norse god Odin killed Thiazi. Skadi then strapped on her skis, gathered up her bow and arrows—she was an excellent archer and hunter, like the Roman goddess Diana (August 7–13)—and set out to avenge her father's murder.

When Skadi reached Asgard, where Odin and his fellow deities lived, the gods tried to appease the angry goddess and avoid further conflict. Odin invited her to marry one of his tribe, known as the Vanir, and become a member of his court. Infatuated with the handsome god Baldur, Skadi agreed, hoping he'd become her husband. There was a catch, however. Skadi had to choose her husband sight unseen from a group of gods—she could only look at their shoes to make her decision. Unfortunately, she picked the sea god Njord, who not only was old and ugly; he also hated the mountains that were Skadi's home. After only two weeks, the marriage dissolved.

Legends vary about what followed. Some say Skadi eventually married Odin, with whom she had a son who became the king of Norway. Others suggest she hooked up with Ullr, the god of winter. Perhaps she chose to remain independent and solitary on her mountaintop, where she continues to ski and hunt alone.

Where to Seek Her

This mountain goddess speaks to us from the high peaks, where winter's winds howl constantly and the snow never melts. If you live in the north, you'll find many icy-cold places at this time of year to seek her counsel. Otherwise, go to an isolated, barren spot and sit in quiet contemplation—in the dark of night, if you feel safe doing so—and listen to Skadi's words of wisdom.

Skadi personifies the darkness and hardships we all endure, symbolized by the cold, bleak, seemingly endless Scandinavian winter and her isolation in the mountains. Despite the harshness of her environment, however, she remains true to herself. Although she's willing to entertain a compromise with Odin and the other Vanir gods, and gives marriage a try, she refuses to relinquish the life she loves to please her husband or his kin.

REASONS TO INVITE HER

Do you feel someone has wronged you, or that you've been treated unfairly? Do you long to see justice done? The culprit punished? Are you seeking vindication or restitution? If so, Skadi can lend you her courage and fervor to stand up to an adversary. She'll teach you how to fight for what's rightfully yours and to trust your inner strength. This athletic goddess can also champion people who enjoy winter sports, especially skiing and snowshoeing.

HOW TO INVITE HER

This practice lets you symbolically melt a hardship, obstacle, or difficulty in your life so that beneficial energy can flow and you can move forward. You'll need:

- *Snow, natural ice, or ice cubes*
- *A glass bowl*
- *Food coloring*

1. On the first day of the week, place a handful of snow or ice into the glass bowl.
2. Assign the snow or ice a problem or obstacle you are facing and want to eliminate.
3. Put a drop of food coloring on the snow or ice. The color should represent the problem; for example, green for money issues, red for anger.

4. Place the bowl in a warm spot and watch the snow/ice melt. As it does, feel Skadi helping you to dissolve the problem. Then pour the water down the drain.

5. Repeat each day of this week. You may choose to melt a different obstacle each day or continue working on the same one until you feel you've completely eliminated it. You can use this practice to solicit Skadi's aid in the future, if you wish.

XI WANGMU

The Chinese New Year is celebrated in late January or early February; therefore, we honor the goddess Xi Wangmu this week. Also known as Wangmu Niangniang, she's one of the oldest of the Chinese deities and often called the Queen Mother of the West.

HERSTORY

Wang translates as "sovereign" or "spirit," and *mu* means "mother." The goddess's name can be interpreted as "grandmother," a title of respect in China for a female ancestor, perhaps one who exists in the spirit world. In a broader sense, Xi Wangmu personifies the feminine creative power in the universe, or yin.

According to some sources, this mother-creator deity was a divine weaver, who wove the cosmos into being—similar to the Norse goddess Frigg (October 2–8) and the Native American goddess Spider Woman (December 25–31). She guides the sun and the moon through the heavens, governs the constellations, and maintains order throughout the universe. Some ancient images show Xi Wangmu holding a loom called a *sheng*. In the *I Ching*, a 3,000-year-old oracle and book of wisdom, *sheng* is expressed as "pushing upward" and is linked with ascension, success, and good fortune. Likewise, the Chinese see Xi Wangmu as a beneficent goddess who showers her people with health, wealth, and happiness. Like a good mother, she protects and nourishes her followers and all things on our planet.

Symbols and Correspondences

One of the many stories about Xi Wangmu tells us she owns a magnificent garden where rare peach trees grow. The trees produce fruit only once every 3,000 years. Whoever eats one of the goddess's peaches becomes immortal.

In some myths, Xi Wangmu makes her home on the sacred Jade Mountain. Others say her palace is located high in the Kunlun Mountains, which scholar Suzanne Cahill describes as "a mysterious place outside of time, without pain or death, where all pleasures and arts flourished: joyous music, dancing, poetry, and divine feasts." A menagerie of mythic creatures, including dragons and phoenixes, live on the mountain with her and do her bidding. A shapeshifter herself, Xi Wangmu assumes the forms of magic animals for her shamanic journeys.

The majestic and impossibly high mountain may serve as a conduit between the worlds, linking heaven and earth. Once a year, on the seventh hour of the seventh day of the seventh month, the goddess comes down to earth, bringing peace, harmony, and blessings to humankind.

Her Animal Totems

Art and legend often show Xi Wangmu in the company of tigers and leopards. One myth describes her as being mostly human in appearance, but with a tiger's teeth and the tail of a leopard. Others depict her as a tigress with a woman's head. An ancient text says three bluebirds brought her fruit to eat.

REASONS TO INVITE HER

This goddess's creative powers can promote healing, encourage happiness, and stimulate growth in any area. If you're feeling a financial pinch or would just like to have a little extra so you can enjoy life more, call upon this generous creator goddess to help you attract abundance. She can also guide you on your path to success and protect you from pitfalls along the way. If you're uncertain what direction to go, ask Xi Wangmu to reveal your destiny to you. She may even take you on a shamanic journey to visit other realms of existence.

HOW TO INVITE HER

Following the goddess's example, you can weave good things into your life. This prosperity ritual can help you attract financial gain, career success, or other forms of abundance. You'll need:

- *A figurine or picture of a tiger*
- *Sandalwood incense (sandalwood is associated with good luck in China and other parts of Asia)*
- *An incense holder*
- *Matches or a lighter*
- *A pen or marker that writes gold ink*
- *3 (36-inch) red ribbons*
- *3 I Ching coins (Chinese coins with a square cut out in the center, typically used for doing I Ching readings; available in Asian gift shops and online)*

1. Place the tiger figurine or picture on a table or other surface.
2. Fit the incense into the holder and place it beside the tiger. Then light the incense to summon Xi Wangmu.

3. Use your gold pen or marker to write one wish related to abundance on each ribbon. In China, red is considered a fortunate color and three is believed to be a lucky number.
4. When you've finished writing all three wishes, tie the ribbons together at one end.
5. Braid the three ribbons while you hold in your mind a vision of yourself receiving what you desire.
6. Tie an *I Ching* coin at the end of each ribbon.
7. Hang the ribbon braid in the Wealth Gua of your home. To locate this, stand at your front door, looking inside. According to the ancient Chinese art of feng shui, the Wealth Gua is at the far left section of your home.
8. Depending on your circumstances, you may receive good fortune from Xi Wangmu promptly, or it may take a while to manifest.

ATHENA

DATES FOR INVITING HER: *January 22–28*

During the first week of the sun's passage through the zodiac sign Aquarius, we honor the Greek goddess Athena. Aquarius is a mentally oriented sign, and Athena governs intellectual pursuits, including literature and the law. Like many Aquarian people, she's also strong-willed, independent, and a fierce defender of justice.

HERSTORY

Greek myths tell us Athena was the daughter of the top Olympian god, Zeus. She had an unusual birth, however. Instead of coming into the world in the normal manner, she sprang from her father's head. Unlike many other goddesses, the independent Athena didn't marry. She preferred to devote her mental and creative energy to inventing useful things for her people, from ships and chariots to musical instruments. She also taught the Greeks how to weave and make pottery.

Known as a warrior deity, Athena is often depicted wearing battle armor and a helmet and carrying a spear. She protected Athens—the city named for her—from attackers, using strategy and pragmatism. During times of peace, she guided the city-state in matters of law, industry, ethical behavior, and organization. She even gave Athens the olive tree, whose fruit remains a valuable source of revenue for Greece today. The gift won her pride of place as the city's top goddess and patroness.

Many epic tales, including Homer's *Odyssey*, feature Athena as a divine guide and helper. She aided Perseus when he killed the Gorgon Medusa, and she assisted Jason in building his famous ship, the *Argo*.

REASONS TO INVITE HER

In addition to celebrating Athena—and your own wisdom—this week you can summon her for assistance whenever you face an intellectual challenge. If you're taking a test, considering an important career decision, or want to learn a new skill, ask Athena for divine guidance and insight. Call on her to bring justice in a legal matter or other situation, especially if you feel things aren't entirely on the up and up or that you've been treated unfairly. A patroness of independent women, Athena encourages you to seek equity in the workplace, as well as in your relationships, to stand up for yourself and to have confidence in your abilities.

HOW TO INVITE HER

Formulate this special oil and use it anytime you wish to harness Athena's power to improve your mental clarity and concentration. You'll need:

- *3 ounces organic virgin olive oil*
- *1 freshly washed clear glass jar or bottle, with a lid, cap, or cork*
- *3 drops lemon essential oil*
- *3 drops ginger essential oil*
- *Transparent adhesive tape, glue, or rubber band*
- *A picture of an owl, or an owl's feather*

1. Pour the olive oil into the bottle, then add the essential oils. Cap the bottle, then shake three times to blend the mixture.
2. Use tape, glue, or your rubber band to affix the picture of the owl and/or the feather to the bottle.
3. Put a drop of oil on your finger and press it gently on the acupressure point known as Middle of the Person for 1 minute. This point is located in the indentation between the base of your nose and your upper lip, and pressing it improves concentration and memory. (Note: Some people's skin is sensitive to essential oils. If this is true for you, dab some of the oil mixture on a handkerchief and hold it near your nose, so you can smell it while you press your finger to the acupressure point.)
4. Close your eyes and inhale the stimulating scent, while you connect with the energy of the goddess. Feel your mind grow clear and focused.

BRIGID

DATES FOR INVITING HER:
January 29–February 4

This beloved Irish deity's holiday is usually celebrated from the evening of January 31 until February 2. It's also known as Imbolc, Candlemas, and Brigid's Day. *Imbolc* means "in the belly," and this sacred day honors all forms of creativity, those of the mind as well as the body.

HERSTORY

The Celts called her "exalted one." The Catholic Church, when it moved into Ireland, renamed her Saint Brigid because the local people refused to give up their favorite goddess. A fiery deity who warms the world during the dark winter season, Brigid rules both the homemaker's hearth fire and the smith's forge. Thus, she symbolizes both the feminine and masculine forces in nature—and the creative potential inherent in both, which when combined birth everything on our planet.

The element of fire represents inspiration and creativity, and in Celtic lore Brigid presides over this realm. Artists often depict Brigid stirring a bubbling cauldron, in which she blends the physical and spiritual ingredients that nurture us. Cauldrons symbolize the womb and represent fertility. However, legends also link Brigid with Ireland's sacred wells and water. She's the patroness of poets and musicians, as well as healers, teachers, and psychics. An apparent conundrum, Brigid represents the divine union of male and female forces—fire and water, respectively—and thus serves as a symbol of creativity on many levels—mental, spiritual, emotional, and physical. Celebrating Brigid's power recognizes that both masculine and feminine are necessary for manifestation in the material realm.

Her Animal Totems

The early Celts connected Brigid with the cow and the ewe. Both animals played important roles in the lives of Ireland's agrarian people, providing milk as well as meat.

REASONS TO INVITE HER

Call upon Brigid whenever you feel a need for inspiration—when your spirit flags, your imagination hits a wall, or circumstances block your ability to express yourself and your dreams. She can spark new life in creative ventures of all kinds, the spiritual and mental as well as physical ones. A patroness of artists and craftspeople, Brigid can give you confidence in your talents and your ability to express them productively. Ask her to help you understand and unite the fertile forces within you, so that you may bring forth the "child" that is your gift to the world.

HOW TO INVITE HER

During Brigid's festival week, enact this ritual that combines candles and a cauldron to encourage creativity in any area of your life. Ideally, you'll want to begin on the evening of January 31, as your ritual may continue for a couple days. You'll need:

- *A nail, ballpoint pen, or other sharp object*
- *6 candles in colors that represent your intention: pink for love, gold for wealth, green for health, orange for success, blue for serenity, white for protection, red for vitality, etc. You may choose candles of several colors or all of the same color, depending on your intention(s).*
- *A cauldron or large fireproof pot*
- *Sand or kitty litter*
- *Matches or a lighter*

1. Use the nail or other sharp tool to carve your intention (in a word or two) into the candles' wax. You may choose to inscribe all the candles with the same wish or mark each candle with a different objective.
2. Fill the cauldron with sand or kitty litter.
3. After securing each candle in the sand or kitty litter, use your matches or lighter to light it. As you light each candle, call out to Brigid and ask her to assist you in your endeavor.
4. Gaze into the candles' flames and sense the goddess's presence. Feel her offering her help and encouraging you in your creative pursuits. You may see the flames flicker as she responds to your request and gives you the go-ahead.
5. Let the candles burn down completely. If that's not possible, extinguish them and light them again the next day. Continue this ritual daily until the candles have finished burning and you sense the goddess is working with you to accomplish your objectives.

"With the lengthening days which distinguish the third month of winter from its predecessor, come ardent desires for spring, and longing for the time of birds and flowers."

—Oscar Fay Adams, American author and editor

FEBRUARY

Although winter still holds parts of the earth in its frozen grip, hope and anticipation have begun stirring within us. This month the goddesses Saraswati, Lilith, Nut, and Aurora sing promises of creativity, sensuality, and the renewal that is sure to come. You'll meet them here and hear their stories of self-expression, ingenuity, and inspiration. If you're experiencing challenges or frustration, if you seek more freedom or knowledge, let them show you how to trust yourself and let your light shine bright.

SARASWATI

We honor Saraswati, the Hindu goddess of knowledge, this week. In India, her festival, Vasant Panchami, is celebrated during the Hindu month of Magha, in late January or February. Hindus mark her holiday by teaching children to read and write. Schools and universities honor her with prayer rituals known as *pujas*. People dress in yellow clothing and eat saffron rice, because yellow is said to be the goddess's favorite color.

HERSTORY

A creator deity in Hindu mythology, Saraswati is associated with all flowing things, including the flow of words. Mythology tells us she gave human beings the ability to speak. Although she's considered a Hindu deity, the Jains (followers of a religion popular in India and noted for its emphasis on nonviolence) and some Buddhists honor her too. This goddess governs knowledge in its many forms: language, poetry, art, music, and science. Some artists portray Saraswati holding a lotus in one of her hands, a symbol of divine wisdom.

Saraswati personifies the idea that knowledge is power, and that knowledge should be shared and used for the good of all. To that end, she facilitates the flow of knowledge between the divine realm and the human world. She's even considered the mother of the ancient body of religious literature known as the Vedas. Her brilliance dispels confusion and ignorance, and she signifies pure wisdom.

According to myth, Saraswati was married to the god Brahma and together they created the universe. Initially, however, the cosmos was in a state of complete chaos, with no structure or order. Brahma felt perplexed at the enormity of the task facing him. But the wise and beautiful goddess Saraswati held the key to establishing order: knowledge. She helped her husband understand the power of mantras, sound, and music and taught him to use them to generate creative energy, or prana. From this energy the earth and the heavens emerged, and life as we know it evolved.

Symbols and Correspondences

Called the "flowing one," Saraswati has dominion over rivers, including the river of consciousness. Often she plays a *veena* (a type of lute), and when she appears with four arms rather than the usual two her hands also hold a book and a *mala* (prayer beads).

REASONS TO INVITE HER

This goddess of knowledge can assist you with any intellectual endeavor, whether you want to learn a new subject, put together a business proposal, or write a novel. Saraswati is a patroness of artistic people—her skill in music, poetry, and art can inspire you to be more imaginative. She'll serve as your muse by dissolving creative blocks and boosting your self-confidence. The goddess can also help you bring structure and clarity into a disorganized situation, perhaps by teaching you to use mantras and meditation to still your mind so you can see solutions to problems.

Her Animal Totems

Sometimes Saraswati is depicted with two companions: a swan, which symbolizes purity and knowledge, and a peacock, whose colorful plumage represents the arts over which she presides.

HOW TO INVITE HER

On Vasant Panchami, people in India celebrate Saraswati. You, too, can pay homage to the goddess and request her blessings in the coming year. If possible, read to children this week or attend/organize a children's reading event at a library or school. If that's not an option, try the following ritual to connect with the goddess:

1. Read a book that focuses on a subject you want to learn more about or one that presents an idea with which you aren't familiar. It may be fiction, nonfiction, poetry—whatever piques your interest. Saraswati encourages you to expand your range of knowledge and explore new ideas.

2. When you've finished, write a brief summary of the book and explain what you got out of reading it. How did it engage you? What did you learn? Do you feel intrigued to learn more? Did the book open new avenues to you or cause you to think about things differently? Did the activity bring you into closer awareness of Saraswati and help you appreciate her guidance more?

3. Get together with other people to discuss the book(s) you read this week. Describe what you found thought-provoking, informative, or inspiring. Saraswati urges you to share your knowledge with others and to learn from them as well. Do you sense her guiding your discussions?

4. At the close of your get-together, give the book you read to someone else you think might enjoy it. If you prefer, donate the book to your local library or another outlet that supports literacy. By giving the gift of knowledge to others, you echo the goddess's intention: to share wisdom with one and all.

LILITH

Perhaps the earliest feminist, the Hebrew goddess Lilith personifies traits astrologers associate with Aquarius, the zodiac sign in which the sun is positioned this week. Those traits include independence, a desire for equality, and a thirst for knowledge.

HERSTORY

Mythology tells us that Lilith was Adam's first wife, although revisionists excised her from the Bible for her audacious insistence on being considered equal to her husband. Unlike Eve, Lilith was created at the same time and from the same stuff as Adam, therefore she saw no reason to play second fiddle to him. She also demanded equality in sex and refused to lie beneath Adam. The couple's inability to compromise led Lilith to leave Paradise—or perhaps a patriarchal god banished her.

Either way, Lilith royally riled the Jewish and Christian fathers, who then set about to vilify her for all time. When she's spoken of now, she's usually described as a demon. Much of her story, as we hear it today, dates back to the *Alphabet of Ben Sira*, written in the eighth century C.E. According to this work, Lilith supposedly mated with the angel of death, known as

Samael, and produced a hundred babies each day—babies the Old Testament God threatened to murder unless she relented, shamefaced, and returned to Eden. She responded by killing human babies. This story took hold and evolved in Christian mythology, eventually casting Lilith as a monster who devoured children as well as other people she didn't like.

Lilith's story didn't arise full-blown in Judeo-Christian mythology, however. We see connections to her in the more ancient goddess Inanna in Sumerian legends, including one that says Lilith took up residence in a sacred *huluppu* tree that grew in Inanna's garden.

Where to Seek Her

In the last half-century, contemporary women have embraced Lilith as a symbol of independence and equality. Therefore, you're likely to find her today among women's groups who are working to bring about parity in the workplace or who support women's rights in health-related areas.

REASONS TO INVITE HER

Do you feel you aren't being treated fairly at home or in the workplace? Do you worry that your intimate partner doesn't respect you as an equal? In your job, are you subjected to unwanted sexual advances or discrimination based on your gender? If so, let Lilith show you how to stand up for yourself.

The goddess's understanding of feminine sexuality can also help you fulfill your own sexual needs and to shuck off old, outworn ideas about how women should behave—in the bedroom and elsewhere. Lilith can teach you the art of sex magic and ecstatic sex, and how to claim the creative power it offers. She'll shift your thinking, so you experience sex as a sacred activity, not merely a brief and simple pleasure. She'll guide and encourage you as you plumb your sensual depths and discover the primal power you have at your disposal. Not only will you enjoy greater passion and pleasure; you'll connect with the innate creative force that lies within you.

HOW TO INVITE HER

Invite Lilith to join you in the bedroom, where she can ramp up your sex life and introduce you to the secrets of ancient sex magic rites. The Greeks enacted sacred sex rituals 5,000 years ago, during which priestesses embodied the Goddess in the act of Divine Marriage. But many other cultures and spiritual schools around the world also engaged in fertility rites as a way to access the Divine and to generate results in the material world. If you're new to these ideas, take some time to study the traditions, concepts, rituals, and purposes before engaging in intimate activity, either with a partner or solo.

When you feel comfortable exploring this powerful practice, ask Lilith to participate in your sex rituals—all you need to do is invite her to join you.

Her Animal Totems

According to legend, Lilith could shapeshift into an owl, symbol of wisdom. An ancient Sumerian sculpture shows her with the wings and feet of an owl, and a reference in the Old Testament book of Isaiah translates *lilith* as "screech owl." She's also linked with serpents, which represent occult knowledge. One story says she took the form of a snake in order to share her knowledge with Adam's second wife in the Garden of Eden.

NUT

DATES FOR INVITING HER: *February 19–25*

In ancient times, the Egyptians honored the sky goddess Nut shortly before the new solar year began on the spring equinox, during what we now think of as late February. One of the oldest deities in Egyptian mythology, she's credited with having brought about the 365-day calendar year (although originally it didn't start on January 1).

HERSTORY

Myth tells us that this beautiful goddess, who presided over the sky and all the celestial bodies held within it, was married to the Egyptian earth god, Geb. Artists and myths often depict her as a dark blue nude woman emblazoned with stars, arched over Geb as the sky arches over the earth. Together they symbolize the integral relationship between our planet and the heavens.

When Nut became pregnant, her father, Ra, the sun god, worried that her offspring might overthrow him, as sometimes happened in the realm of the deities. To prevent this, he forbade the goddess to have a child on any day of the year. At that time, Egypt's calendar only had 360 days. Nut's predicament seemed impossible—until the clever god Thoth found a way around the dilemma. Instead of directly confronting Ra, Thoth invited the moon god, Khonsu, to play a gambling game, during which he beat Khonsu out of enough moonlight to create five days beyond the original 360. Nut, then, was allowed to give birth to one child on each of the new days.

Where to Seek Her

Go outside at night when the sky is full of stars and gaze up at the Milky Way. Feel your connection with the heavens and with Nut. You can also look for this goddess in the evening as the sun sets and at dawn when it rises again.

Another legend says Nut created the days and nights. Reputedly, this sky goddess swallowed the sun at the end of each day and birthed it again each morning. Therefore, she represents the ongoing cycle of birth, death, and rebirth.

REASONS TO INVITE HER

Mythology describes Nut as a creator goddess, whose children were some of Egypt's best-known deities. She also had the awesome responsibility of controlling the cycle of day and night. Additionally, she's said to guide and protect souls on their way to the afterlife—the Egyptians petitioned her assistance by painting her picture on the inside lids of sarcophagi.

Symbols and Correspondences

Some images of Nut show her balancing a pot of water on her head, which may represent the womb. You can set a pot of water outside at night and let it reflect the heavenly bodies shining in the sky, while you wish upon a star.

Nut's power can help women who wish to become pregnant, or people who want to birth any type of creative endeavor. If someone you love has passed, this goddess who was known as the Friend of the Dead offers solace and reminds you that your loved one is safe in her arms. If you've experienced another type of loss, ask Nut to show you how to make a comeback, just as the sun returns each morning after a period of darkness.

HOW TO INVITE HER

To petition the goddess's favor this week, begin the following ritual on February 19 after the sun has gone down and night has settled in. She'll help you get started with any kind of creative endeavor. You'll need:

- *A dark blue candle*
- *A candleholder*
- *Matches or a lighter*
- *A pen, pencil, or marker that writes dark blue ink*
- *A piece of paper*
- *3 star sapphires or other dark blue gemstones (such as sodalite, blue fluorite, or lapis lazuli)*
- *A dark blue cloth*

1. Place the candle in the candleholder and light it.
2. By the candle's light use the blue pen (or pencil or marker) to write what you desire from the goddess on the paper. State your request in a positive way; for example, "Nut, bring me success in my new business," and hold in your mind an image of your wish coming true.
3. Lay the piece of paper on a table or other surface.
4. Set the three gemstones that represent the night sky on the piece of paper.
5. Cover everything except the candle with the dark blue cloth. Let the candle burn for up to an hour, then extinguish it.

6. Leave everything in place throughout the week. Relight the candle each evening, let it burn for a while, and then extinguish it. Hold the image of your desire being fulfilled as you sense Nut's presence.
7. At the end of the week, burn the paper in a fireplace, barbecue grill, or other safe place and thank the goddess. Collect the stones and store them in a safe place.

AURORA

DATES FOR INVITING HER:
February 26–March 4

Also known as the goddess of the dawn, Aurora personifies hope and new beginnings. This Roman goddess's name means "dawn" or "sunrise" in Latin. Therefore, as the days grow longer and the promise of spring is in the air, we look this week to Aurora to dispel darkness and shine her rosy light on our endeavors.

HERSTORY

Mythology presents Aurora as a beautiful young goddess who rises before anyone else and wakes up her brother, Sol (meaning "sun"), so he can light up the world. She's said to open the gate to heaven each morning and then ride her golden, horse-drawn chariot across the sky. Sometimes Aurora is described as wearing a fuchsia cloak, which colors the morning sky at dawn; other images show her dressed in pink and gold, bedecked with flowers. Because she reawakens each day, the goddess symbolizes renewal and eternal youth.

Not surprisingly, the gorgeous Aurora attracted the attention of many gods, including Mars. This didn't sit well with his jealous lover, Venus, however, and she decided to get revenge. She cast a spell on Aurora that made her fall in love (or at least lust) with mortal men. According to one story, she married a handsome young man named Tithonus. Goddesses are immortal, and Aurora feared the inevitable death of her human husband. She asked the top god, Jupiter, to let Tithonus live forever, but she neglected to specify that he remain forever young—a classic case of be careful what you ask for. As the years passed, Tithonus grew ancient, withered, and decrepit. Saddened by his pathetic state, Aurora pleaded with Jupiter to end Tithonus's suffering. The god turned him into a cicada, and now at dawn he chirps his greeting to the goddess.

Symbols and Correspondences

Legend says the precious golden herb saffron was sacred to Aurora. She was also fond of all flowers, but especially roses. The Roman poet Ovid credited her with creating dew from her tears.

Aurora bears a strong resemblance to the Greeks' Eos because the ancient Romans often grafted their deities onto older ones. Sometimes they combined Aurora with an earlier local goddess, Mater Matuta, who governed childbirth and protected children. In the sixth century B.C.E., Aurora's temple was built in a special area of Rome's Forum, where a number of temples dedicated to various deities once stood. There, mothers worshipped Aurora and petitioned her to guard their children, thanking her with offerings of sacred cakes called *testuacia*.

Where to Seek Her

At the break of dawn, look to the east and watch as the sky shifts from deep purple to pink—some myths say Aurora colors the sky by drawing her rosy fingers across it. As the goddess wakes up the world, she'll shed light on you and bring you hope.

REASONS TO INVITE HER

Are you hoping for a new dawn after a period of difficulty? Aurora reminds us that darkness doesn't last forever and shows the way to brighter days ahead. Dawn's pure light chases away shadows, enabling you to see matters more clearly. The goddess also helps you awaken to your potential, to "rise and shine" and face each day with the optimism of youth. She encourages you to try something new, perhaps a new romance, a new job, or a new place to live. Whatever you embark on, summon the goddess to illuminate your path.

HOW TO INVITE HER

The lovely Aurora had no trouble attracting lovers—divine and mortal. If you seek a new romantic partner, ask her to help bring you the person who's right for you in every way. You can also summon Aurora to attract anything you'll love, such as a fulfilling job or the perfect pet. You'll need:

- *A piece of pink paper*
- *A pen, pencil, or marker that writes red ink*
- *Scissors*
- *2 dark pink rose petals*
- *A pinch of saffron*
- *Transparent adhesive tape*

1. Rise at dawn.
2. On the pink paper draw a heart with your red pen/pencil/marker, and then cut it out.
3. Write your intention on the paper heart, stating the outcome you seek in a positive way. As you work, envision your wish coming true and sense Aurora helping you to achieve your heart's desire.
4. Lay the rose petals and saffron, an herb long associated with the sun's life-giving power, in the center of the paper heart, then fold it closed and secure it with tape.
5. Sleep with the heart under your pillow each night this week, then store it in a safe place.

"By March, the worst of the winter would be over. The snow would thaw, the rivers begin to run and the world would wake into itself again."

—Neil Gaiman, English author, *Odd and the Frost Giants*

MARCH

In March the dark days are behind us, and everywhere we look we see beauty beginning to emerge. This month the goddesses Kuan Yin, Sedna, Ostara, and Tiamat encourage us to embrace a new cycle of creativity. Here you'll get to know these goddesses and hear their stories. You'll learn how to draw on their experiences in order to dispel darkness in your own life and see the world in a new light. Spring opens the door to infinite possibilities.

KUAN YIN

DATES FOR INVITING HER: *March 5–11*

This week we honor the goddess Kuan Yin, who's sometimes considered the feminine equivalent of the Buddha. Traditionally, the Chinese celebrate her feast on the nineteenth day of the second lunar month, which varies year to year but usually occurs between February 21 and March 20.

HERSTORY

Beloved in China and many parts of Eastern Asia, Kuan Yin (also spelled Quan Yin, Guanyin, and Kannon) is considered a bodhisattva, a holy one who took pity on humankind and returned to earth to help them, rather than entering Nirvana. *Kuan* means "earth," and *yin* refers to the feminine life force. Her Sanskrit name, *Padmapani*, means "born of the lotus," and this gentle goddess often appears floating on a white lotus blossom, which represents her purity. She also has dominion over the animals and nature.

According to one legend, Kuan Yin is the reincarnation of the Buddha. Another says that more than 2,500 years ago the goddess took on a human form as a princess and Buddhist nun named Miao Shan, who cared for the poor, sick, and dying. Sometimes she's portrayed with a thousand arms and eyes on her hands that enable her to see and give aid to all who are suffering.

Kuan Yin offers both peace and protection to those in need, especially women and children. She's also a patroness of seafarers. Myths tell us she lived on the mountainous island P'u-t'o Shan in the East China Sea for nine years, where she rescued shipwrecked sailors; the island is still considered a sacred pilgrimage site for her followers.

Her Animal Totems

As guardian of the animal kingdom, Kuan Yin is sometimes shown on the back of a dolphin or fish, symbols of the water element and the universal feminine force (yin). She's also portrayed riding an elephant or a lion, or in the company of dragons, which signify her power and wisdom.

REASONS TO INVITE HER

Kuan Yin personifies kindness, compassion, and mercy. If you tend to be too hard on yourself or harbor guilt about something, let the goddess pour her divine water over you to wash away self-judgment. If you think someone has wronged you, Kuan Yin can help you open your heart and forgive that person. Remember, forgiveness isn't the same as condoning—it releases attachments that keep you bound to the wheel of karma (in Buddhist belief). The epitome of serenity, Kuan Yin can show you how to find peace, even amid the stress and confusion of everyday life.

HOW TO INVITE HER

If you want Kuan Yin to grant you serenity, compassion, loving-kindness, forgiveness, or protection, this ritual will help you invite the goddess into your life. You'll ideally want to use a figurine of the goddess—jade, ivory, and bronze are traditional—but if those options aren't feasible you can purchase one of a less costly material or download a picture of her from an online site. You'll need:

- *A pretty Chinese shawl or a white cloth*
- *A likeness of Kuan Yin*
- *A lotus flower*
- *A bowl of water*
- *Incense*
- *An incense holder*
- *Matches or a lighter*

1. Spread the shawl or cloth on a table or other surface where you can leave it for the entire week.
2. Position the likeness of Kuan Yin on the shawl or cloth.
3. Float the lotus blossom in the bowl of water and set it to the left of the image of the goddess.
4. Fit the incense into the holder and place it to the right of the image of the goddess.
5. Light the incense. Buddhists say burning incense invokes the essence of the deity into the figurine or other likeness.
6. Ask the goddess to grant you serenity, compassion, loving-kindness, forgiveness, protection, or whatever you seek.
7. Let the incense finish burning, then thank Kuan Yin for being with you and offering her assistance.
8. Repeat the ritual each day of this week to attract Kuan Yin's blessings.

Symbols and Correspondences

Artists usually show this compassionate deity holding a vessel aloft, pouring holy water—the water of kindness—on humankind to wash away their misery, dissolve suffering, and promote healing. Sometimes Kuan Yin also holds a willow branch or a sheaf of rice with which she drips sacred nectar onto the earth to nourish it.

SEDNA

At this time of year, we see how that which died during the winter months has made possible the new life that will nourish us in the future. Sedna, the most important of the Inuit goddesses, represents sacrifice and nourishment, death and rebirth. This week, therefore, we honor this goddess of transformation.

HERSTORY

According to Inuit legend, Sedna once lived on the shores of the Arctic Ocean as a mortal woman—and a beautiful one at that. She had a willful streak, however, and refused to marry any of the suitable young men in her village who sought her hand. Instead, she eloped with a mysterious stranger who turned out to be a seagull (or fulmar) in disguise. Although he'd promised her a life of luxury, Sedna found herself isolated on a bleak island populated only by seabirds.

One day her father came to visit, and the unhappy Sedna begged him to take her back home. When he tried to paddle away with her, an angry flock of birds pursued their kayak, whipping up a storm with their wings. In a panic, Sedna's father threw his daughter overboard.

The frightened girl tried to climb back into the kayak, but her father chopped off her fingers.

As she sunk beneath the water's surface, Sedna morphed into an unusual sea creature, with the head and torso of a woman and the scaly tail of a fish—a mermaid. Her severed fingers transformed into seals, whales, narwhals, and other aquatic beings. She took up residence at the bottom of the ocean, which Inuit folklore tells us is where the deities live. Thus Sedna was elevated to the role of goddess and the mother of all marine life, which makes up the majority of the Inuit diet.

This creator goddess continues to provide abundant game for the Inuit to eat, but only so long as they pay her the respect she deserves as their protector and benefactor. When she grows angry, she sends fierce storms that prevent the people from going out to hunt. To calm her down, shamans visit Sedna in her ocean home and comb her long black hair, for without fingers she can't do this herself.

Where to Seek Her

Legends say Sedna lives in the land of Adlivun, at the bottom of the Arctic Ocean. However, you can seek her in any body of water: a lake or pond, a stream or river, or the ocean. Her underwater realm also can represent your own unconscious.

REASONS TO INVITE HER

Sedna's story is a tale of transformation—something must die so that something else can live. When you have to let go of an old, familiar way of being and move bravely into the unknown, invite this goddess to accompany you. If you find it necessary to sacrifice something for the good of others, let Sedna show you how to offer this gift with grace and humility. She'll also help you transcend the ego and discover the benevolent goddess within you.

HOW TO INVITE HER

We often associate water with the emotions. The sea goddess, Sedna, can assist you in dealing with an emotional issue and guide you to a place of peace. You'll need:

- *An image of a mermaid*
- *A piece of tree bark about 4–6 inches long*
- *A pen or marker that will write on the bark*

1. Set the image of the mermaid on the table before you, to represent Sedna.
2. On the smooth side of the piece of bark, write your request to the goddess. As you write, envision her presence, giving you strength and insight.
3. Draw images of fish, seals, whales, or other sea creatures on the bark. Think about how they navigate their environment with ease. Can you learn from their example?
4. When you've finished, take the piece of bark to a body of water.
5. Set the bark in the water and let it float, like a boat, on the surface. Watch as it drifts away, carrying your wish to the goddess.
6. Say a prayer to Sedna and ask her to help bring about the outcome you desire.
7. Place the image of the mermaid in a spot where you'll see it often.

Friends and Foes

Aquatic creatures were Sedna's children and sacred to her. Birds, on the other hand, tricked, imprisoned, and attacked her. In myths and dreams, water symbolizes the intuition, whereas air represents the intellect. Her legend, therefore, may describe a conflict between two ways of receiving and processing information.

OSTARA

On the spring equinox, and during the first week of spring in the Northern Hemisphere, we honor the Germanic fertility goddess Ostara or Eostre (from which our word *Easter* comes). Her holiday signifies a turning point in the solar year, after which daylight will last longer than nighttime.

HERSTORY

Spring is a time of awakening and renewal, and Ostara brings hope after the long, barren winter season. Folklore sometimes refers to her as the goddess of the dawn, for sunrise chases away the darkness and blesses the world with new possibilities.

Ostara often appears as a beautiful young woman, radiant with optimism and joie de vivre. One of the Brothers Grimm, Jacob, described her as "the divinity of the radiant dawn, of upspringing light, a spectacle that brings joy and blessing." Artists depict the goddess decked out in flowers that blossom at this time of the year. New life bursts forth on earth now, birdsong fills the air, and baby animals are born. Farmers till and sow their fields as the time of fertility begins.

You, too, can plant seeds symbolically this week as your own creative juices start to stir. Ostara inspires you to express your vision, to awaken to the promise and abundance that lie within you, and to begin new projects that will bear fruit in the coming months.

> ### Her Animal Totems
>
> The popular practice of decorating eggs at Easter derives from a legend told about Ostara. During winter, the goddess found a half-frozen bird lying on the cold ground. She changed it into a rabbit and thereby saved its life. However, the rabbit retained some of its bird qualities, including the ability to lay eggs. To thank the goddess, the rabbit painted some eggs for her. Ostara liked them so much she told the rabbit to give them to everyone in the world. Of course, we associate both eggs and rabbits with fertility.

REASONS TO INVITE HER

Invite Ostara at the start of a new venture—she'll lend you her exuberance and fertilize your efforts. If you feel stumped or frustrated in a creative endeavor, or can't seem to get an undertaking off the ground, ask Ostara for inspiration and guidance. Like the bird she rescued in a legend, the goddess will nurture you and revive your self-confidence. You can also call on her for help planting an herb, vegetable, or flower garden.

HOW TO INVITE HER

Celebrate Ostara this week by decorating eggs to thank her for the abundance in your life and to request her continued assistance in the coming year. You'll need:

- *5 pots of water, large enough to cook the vegetables (1 pot for each color dye)*
- *1 head red cabbage, chopped (for red dye)*
- *A few beets, sliced (for purple dye)*

- *Skins from a few yellow onions (for yellow dye)*
- *1 large carrot, chopped (for orange dye)*
- *1 large handful fresh spinach (for green dye)*
- *A colander or large sieve*
- *5 glass bowls (1 for each color dye)*
- *10 tablespoons white vinegar, divided*
- *12 large white eggs, hard-boiled*
- *Nontoxic paints or crayons (optional)*

1. In each of the pots, add the vegetable matter for one color and cook until the water is brightly colored.
2. Using the colander or sieve, strain the colored liquid into the bowls and add 2 tablespoons of white vinegar to each bowl to set the dye.
3. Soak the eggs in the colors of your choice, making sure that the liquid covers the eggs completely. The longer the eggs soak, the deeper the color will be.
4. If you like, you can paint or draw images on the eggs that symbolize what you hope to attract: hearts for love, dollar signs for wealth, etc. (Be careful when handling freshly dyed eggs, as some of the dye will rub off.)
5. Later, when you eat the eggs, imagine incorporating their creative potential into your body and materializing whatever you desire.
6. Bury the colorful shells—don't just dump them in the trash—to continue the cycle of fertility and blessings.

Where to Seek Her

To commune with this fertility goddess, take a trip to a farm where the first crops are beginning to poke their green shoots through the soil. Place your palms on the rich earth and sense the vitality of new life bursting forth. If that's not possible, visit a garden center and walk among the rows of budding plants.

TIAMAT

DATES FOR INVITING HER: *March 27–April 2*

The ancient Babylonians celebrated the New Year, known as Akitu, at the first new moon after the spring equinox. The festivities marked the start of the fertile planting season and lasted for eleven days. This week, we honor the Babylonian fertility and mother goddess Tiamat and embrace her creative power as the earth blossoms with new life.

HERSTORY

All cultures and belief systems recount creation myths, and the earliest ones credit goddesses as the origin of All That Is. In Babylonia, that goddess was Tiamat. Usually portrayed as a water dragon, Tiamat personifies the ocean, the fertile source from which modern-day science tells us we evolved. Her name relates to the Babylonian word *tantu*, meaning "sea." Legends describe Tiamat as the mother of everything—not only on earth, but in the divine realm as well. She birthed the celestial bodies and the rest of the gods and goddesses.

This mother goddess, however, bred a family of violently disruptive descendants. When she and Apsu—the god of freshwater—could no longer stand the family discord caused by the younger generations of deities, they decided to get rid of their offspring (eat them, actually). But before they could go through with their plan, Tiamat's great-grandson, Ea, killed Apsu, and Ea's son, Marduk, killed Tiamat by shooting her in the abdomen with an arrow. As she succumbed, water gushed from her eyes, forming the Tigris and Euphrates Rivers that created a stretch of fertile agricultural land in the Middle East known as the Fertile Crescent. According to one telling, Marduk then cut up Tiamat into a number of pieces and used them to make the hills, fields, etc. Thus, even in death, she continued to be a creative force.

Later legends elevated Marduk to the position of supreme god, as a result of having defeated Tiamat. His act of slaying the primordial goddess symbolizes the rise of patriarchy over the earlier matriarchal culture of Babylonia. During the holiday of Akitu, plays were enacted to portray this event in addition to the feasting, partying, and other festive rituals that ushered in the Babylonian planting season.

Where to Seek Her

This goddess of the ocean or "bitter water" abides in saltwater—even in brackish places where myth suggests she and Apsu, her consort, mingled to produce the later deities who ultimately supplanted them. If you have the opportunity to visit an ocean, sea, gulf, or tidal marsh, invite the goddess to join you there.

REASONS TO INVITE HER

Human beings are creative creatures, and the desire to create—though not merely to reproduce biological offspring—propels us toward self-fulfillment. Whatever form our creativity takes, it expresses who we are, what matters to us, and what gifts we have to offer to the world. Do you wish to become more imaginative and productive? Do you long for success in an artistic career? As you embark on a creative venture, ask Tiamat to lend her power to your undertaking, whether that means painting, gardening, writing, cooking, or something else. This dynamic fertility goddess can give you the inspiration and guidance you need to bring your dreams to fruition.

Her Animal Totems

In addition to her usual depiction as a water dragon, Tiamat is sometimes shown with a woman's torso and snaky appendages. As a seawater goddess, she has an affinity with ocean creatures such as eels, dolphins, and crocodiles—she may even appear as a mermaid.

HOW TO INVITE HER

In addition to marking the New Year, Akitu celebrated the beginning of the planting season and the water goddess Tiamat, who nourished the crops and made the soil fertile. The following ritual draws upon the creative power of Tiamat by combining water—a symbol of the Divine Feminine—in its many forms. You'll need:

- *A blue or blue-green glass bottle with a stopper*
- *Saltwater*
- *Spring/freshwater*
- *Water from a source or place you consider sacred*
- *Water from a running stream or river*
- *Rainwater collected during a thunderstorm*
- *Any other forms of water you can gather, such as dew, melted snow, etc.*

1. Cleanse the bottle using organic soap or vinegar and running water.

2. Become aware of Tiamat's presence as you add the various forms of water you've collected, one by one, to the bottle. With each addition, sense the different energies and purposes contained in that type of water.

3. When you've finished adding all the different types of water, cap the bottle, then shake it three times to blend the waters' energies.

4. Sense their disparate natures dissolving and their harmonious properties merging.

5. Empty the bottle of mixed waters outdoors in a place that's dry, rocky, or barren. Sense the goddess blessing this place—and you—with her creative power.

"April hath put a spirit of youth in everything."

—William Shakespeare, English author, "Sonnet 98"

APRIL

April is a time of awakening, of hope and possibilities. Its vibrancy flows through all of nature, enlivening human, animal, bird, plant, and insect. The goddesses of April—Nike, Inanna, Freya, and Flora—express the youthful beauty, exuberance, sensuality, and optimism that burst into the world with April's arrival. In this section, you'll visit with these deities and share in their sagas of power and passion. If you're seeking motivation to create what you desire or to face challenges and emerge victorious, they'll give you the inspiration you need.

NIKE

DATES FOR INVITING HER: *April 3–9*

The sun is in Aries this week, a sign astrologers associate with contests, combat, and sports. In ancient Greece, Nike was known as the goddess of victory in war and in athletic competitions. Thus it's fitting that we honor Nike this week and request her aid in whatever challenges or conflicts we may be facing.

HERSTORY

According to myth, Nike was a favorite goddess of the chief Olympian, Zeus. Her speed, strength, and courage led him to name her his head charioteer during the war with the Titans. Legends tell us she wheeled through the sky during the battle, bringing food and drink to soldiers embroiled in the fighting. One story says that the brave Nike was the only deity who stayed by Zeus's side when the monster Typhoeus attacked Mount Olympus.

Folklore suggests the goddess valued excellence in mortals and propelled those she considered worthy to the heights of glory. Greek soldiers and athletes believed Nike could confer daring and physical power on them, thereby bringing them victory in any type of competition. Some even thought she'd make them immortal. Naturally, this made her very popular—they all wanted this goddess on their side. Usually artists depict Nike with wings that symbolize her ability to soar to the greatest heights of achievement. Sometimes she holds a shield on which she inscribed the names of the winners of each battle. In modern times, her image graces the Olympics medal.

Friends and Foes

Zeus's daughter Athena (January 22–28) and Nike were friends and allies, according to Greek legends. The two goddesses often appear together in art and myth. Interestingly, when Nike is shown in the company of Athena she sometimes sheds her wings or may perch in Athena's hand.

Because celebrations usually accompany success in a battle or a sporting event, legends also give Nike governance over festivities that extol the champions in any type of competition. Whenever athletes clinch the World Series, Super Bowl, or World Cup, you can be sure Nike is there raising her glass in a toast.

REASONS TO INVITE HER

Are you engaged in an athletic contest? A challenge in your workplace or the business world? Is competition moving into your territory, personally or professionally? If so, summon Nike and ask her to bolster your courage and determination, so you can achieve the victory you seek.

Even if the battle is with a part of yourself—a fear or perceived weakness, perhaps, or a behavior that interferes with your success—Nike can boost your confidence. She can also help you achieve recognition for your accomplishments. If you're an athlete or in the military, invite Nike to be your patroness as our ancestors did millennia ago.

HOW TO INVITE HER

This week, perform the following ritual to petition Nike's aid—ask her for protection and success in a competition. You'll need:

- *9 or more dried bay laurel leaves*
- *A gold-colored drawstring pouch, preferably silk*
- *A white feather*
- *A piece of bloodstone (a green stone flecked with red that ancient Greek soldiers carried into battle for courage and protection)*

1. Form a circle on the floor with the bay laurel leaves. The circle should be large enough that you can stand inside it.
2. Step into the circle, close your eyes, and state your request to the goddess.
3. Open your heart and mind to Nike. Sense her presence as she agrees to assist you. You may feel a tingling sensation on the top of your head, as if she were crowning you the winner.
4. When you're confident that Nike has sided with you, step out of the circle and collect the laurel leaves.
5. Place nine of the leaves in the gold-colored pouch. (Save the rest for cooking—Nike's energy will infuse whatever dish you prepare.)
6. Add the feather and the bloodstone.
7. Tie the pouch closed and carry it with you as you meet your competition.

INANNA

DATES FOR INVITING HER: *April 10–16*

This week we honor the Sumerian goddess Inanna, who later appears in Assyrian mythology as Ishtar. She's linked with the rainy season in Mesopotamia, which occurs between November and April. The ancients revered her as the divine embodiment of beauty, fertility, love, and sexuality; therefore, she also epitomizes the lush, vibrant energy of spring.

HERSTORY

According to millennia-old myths, the fertility goddess Inanna, aka the queen of heaven, nourished crops and brought abundance to Mesopotamia. Each year during the rainy season, Sumerian legend says, she mated with her consort, Dumuzi, an act of sympathetic magic intended to bring fertility to the land. This powerful goddess governed all plant and animal growth—without her, life on earth couldn't exist.

However, the beautiful Inanna, whom artists sometimes picture with wings, was notoriously vain, arrogant, and self-centered. She indulged in all sorts of pleasures and wallowed in luxury. And why wouldn't she, given the adoration and infinite blessings that were divinely hers to enjoy? Unfortunately, the queen of heaven had a sister who ruled the underworld: Ereshkigal, queen of the dead. As the story goes, Ereshkigal summoned Inanna to visit the underworld—but this wasn't a friendly family get-together. When Inanna arrived at her sister's palace, she was forced to pass through seven gates to reach Ereshkigal's inner sanctum, and at each gate she was required to sacrifice jewelry, clothing, or other prized possessions. Finally, humbled and naked, Inanna stood before her sister, who, according to some accounts, killed her and hung her body on a hook. Myths disagree about whether Ereshkigal was jealous of her sister or sought retribution for a crime she believed Inanna had committed.

Symbols and Correspondences

Legends show Inanna holding a sacred bundle of reeds, which signifies her divine governance of nature and agriculture, twisted to form a spiral, representing the life force. One myth says the goddess transformed the bundle into a boat when another deity threatened to flood the earth and destroy humankind.

The earth grieved for the fertility goddess, however, and nothing grew—a story we see echoed in the better-known Greek tale of Demeter (September 18–24) and Persephone. Famine spread across the land. To prevent total devastation, Dumuzi exchanged himself for Inanna's freedom, and Ereshkigal allowed her sister to leave the underworld.

REASONS TO INVITE HER

Inanna teaches you to confront your dark side with courage and honesty. To become whole, you may need to give up possessions, attitudes, or behaviors to which you're attached. Are you compromising yourself for reasons of status, comfort, or security? Ask the goddess to help you face your fears and discover your inner strength. She'll show you how to love the parts of yourself that may not be pretty, in order to restore your sense of self and establish balance in your life.

HOW TO INVITE HER

This week examine the hidden parts of yourself—how can bringing them into your awareness facilitate wholeness and growth? Invite Inanna to guide you through the seven "gates" known as the chakras, the vital energy centers in your body through which wisdom and healing enter. (You can find diagrams of the chakras online.) As you direct your attention to each chakra during this ritual, pay attention to insights, impressions, and emotions that awaken within you. You needn't try to analyze or fix problematic situations at this time—simply be aware.

1. On day one, focus on matters related to the root chakra, including your family of origin, security, and self-preservation.
2. On day two, pay attention to things concerning the sacral chakra, such as sexuality, creativity, and financial matters.
3. On day three, notice things associated with the solar plexus chakra, including self-esteem and personal power.
4. On day four, consider issues related to the heart chakra, including love, relationships, and self-acceptance.
5. On day five, focus on matters involving the throat chakra, such as self-expression, honesty, and the exchange of ideas.
6. On day six, connect with issues associated with the brow chakra: intuition, insight, and imagination.
7. On day seven, turn your attention to the crown chakra, which connects you to higher levels of awareness, divine wisdom, and your spirit guides.

FREYA

The Norse goddess Freya is both a fiery war deity and a goddess of sexual passion. Thus we honor her this week, which straddles the zodiac signs Aries and Taurus—both of which astrologers associate with sexuality. Aries is ruled by Mars, the planet of desire, and Taurus is ruled by Venus, planet of love and sensuality.

HERSTORY

According to Norse legend, Freya is the patroness of soldiers. When valiant warriors die in combat, the goddess guides half of them into her afterlife realm known as Fólkvangr, meaning "field of armies." The other half go to the god Odin's wondrous golden hall Valhalla, meaning "hall of the fallen." Although she hails from a family of deities known as the Vanir, Freya was invited to join Odin's opposition clan, called the Aesir, after she negotiated a truce between the two tribes in the legendary Aesir–Vanir war.

In her role as a sex goddess, Freya taught her priestesses the dance of ecstasy, which did more than raise ardor—it also gave them the power of divination. Freya herself was a noted seer with unparalleled knowledge, which should be no surprise considering that she was the one who wove the web of destiny—which governed earthly events—by engaging in the Norse magical art *seidr*. Whenever she wanted to change the course of events, Freya reworked fate by weaving new situations into the original pattern. Reputedly she taught this form of magic to both deities and humans. Some legends also credit her with bringing art and beauty to the world.

Her Animal Totems

In art and myth, Freya is shown riding through the sky in a chariot drawn by two blue-gray cats. Falcons are favorites of hers as well—she wears a magic cape made of falcon feathers that enables her to fly or to shape-shift into a falcon.

REASONS TO INVITE HER

Let Freya show you how to celebrate your beauty and sensuality this week. If your love life has lost its luster, this passionate goddess can give you inspiration. If you don't feel desirable or don't believe you deserve to be admired, Freya can reduce self-judgment and let you appreciate yourself more fully. Call on this strong-willed warrior goddess when you feel unappreciated or powerless in a romantic relationship—she'll teach you how to claim the respect you're due. If you're involved in a contentious partnership, ask Freya to show you how to assert yourself in positive ways without wounding your mate or damaging what's good between you. She can also help you attract abundance by boosting your sense of self-worth.

Symbols and Correspondences

This beautiful goddess loves jewelry and all sorts of luxurious goodies. One story says Freya desired the fabled Brisingamen necklace made of precious metals and gems including gold and amber (*Brisingamen* means "fiery" or "glowing"). To acquire this valuable torque, she traded sexual favors to the dwarfs who'd fashioned it.

HOW TO INVITE HER

This practice, known as casting a glamour, lets you create an illusion that temporarily influences people's perceptions of you and makes you more attractive to them. Invite Freya to guide and assist you and show you her secrets as you engage in this ritual. Because a glamour only lasts for a few hours or so, perform this ritual shortly before going out into the world when you want to make a positive impression. You'll need:

- *2 pink candles*
- *2 candleholders*
- *Matches or a lighter*
- *A mirror, preferably a full-length one*

1. Place the candles in the candleholders, then light the candles and set them in a safe place near the mirror. Turn off all other lights.
2. Stand in front of the mirror and focus on one feature that you find attractive, instead of the things you consider imperfections.
3. As you observe this feature, give yourself some compliments— most of us are too quick to criticize ourselves and can really use a bit of praise.
4. Expand your attention so that you lavish praise on your whole body. Tell yourself how amazing and desirable you are.
5. Sense your aura growing bigger and brighter—you might even feel a slight tingling on your skin or hear an electric crackling around you.
6. Envision divine beauty pouring down over you, like liquid gold. Mentally massage this goddess energy into your aura, so that it merges with your own energy field.
7. Continue doing this as long as you like. Enjoy the feeling. Then extinguish the candles and go out into the world. Notice how other people respond to you.

FLORA

DATES FOR INVITING HER: *April 24–30*

This week, at the height of springtime, we honor Flora, the Roman goddess of flowers, although her worship actually predates the Roman Empire. Her festival, known as Floralia, begins on April 27. The ancient Sabines, a tribe who lived near Rome, celebrated this fertility goddess for the entire month of April, when the land blossomed with colorful flowers.

HERSTORY

According to mythology, this beautiful spring goddess not only presided over flowers, but was also responsible for all crops that blossomed. She encouraged plants to bloom abundantly and protected them against insect pests, diseases, and harm of all kinds. In early agrarian culture, Flora was held in high esteem, for a bountiful harvest depended on her efforts and goodwill. Thus she's associated with fertility and abundance. One legend says that when the goddess Juno wanted to become pregnant, Flora gave her a flower that did the trick. The pregnancy, which some stories say occurred without the necessity of a male, produced the god Mars.

Flora's festival celebrates beauty, sex, and fertility—the end of cold weather, rebirth, and renewal. The ancient Romans marked Floralia with games, chariot races, singing and dancing, and various amusements that had sexual themes. Flora's followers offered gifts of wheat, milk, and honey to the goddess. Revelers scattered flowers in her honor. Girls and young women dressed in colorful clothing and wore headdresses or garlands of flowers.

REASONS TO INVITE HER

Want more love, joy, and abundance in your life? This beautiful goddess can help you attract wealth, improve your sex life, become pregnant, or be more creative. In short, she'll show you how to blossom. If you've experienced a period of drought, Flora offers hope and encourages brighter, more bountiful times ahead. As the goddess of flowers, Flora lends her assistance to gardeners, horticulturists, farmers, botanists, and healers who work with plant medicine. She can teach you how to speak the language of flowers and communicate with the *devas*, the nature spirits that abide in plants and maintain them. If you want to learn herbalism, ask Flora to be your teacher.

Symbols and Correspondences

Naturally, Flora loves flowers of all kinds—especially those that blossom at this time of the year—as well as flowering trees that bear fruit, such as apples, pears, and peaches. Honey, which is made from flowers, and bees are among her favorite things too.

HOW TO INVITE HER

With this prosperity potion you invite Flora to bring you abundance of all kinds and to make your life more fruitful and fulfilling. Begin on the first day of this week and continue daily for seven days. Replace the flowers with fresh ones when they begin to wilt. You'll need:

- *A light green cloth*
- *A vase full of colorful spring flowers*
- *3 different fruit juices (3 is the number of creativity)*
- *Ginger ale (or sparkling water and fresh, grated ginger)*
- *Honey*
- *A glass pitcher or jar*
- *A spoon, preferably silver or silver plate*
- *A pretty goblet or tumbler*

1. Dress in colorful clothing. If you like, wear flowers in your hair.
2. Spread the light green cloth on a table and set the vase of flowers on it.
3. Pour the three fruit juices, ginger ale, and a little honey into a pitcher or jar, while you envision abundance of all kinds coming to you. (Ginger speeds up action and brings faster results.) You may want to add some edible flowers, such as violets or nasturtiums.
4. Use the spoon to stir the mixture three times as you ask Flora to help you acquire what you desire. See the potion sparkle with the goddess's energy.
5. Pour some of the potion into the goblet or tumbler and sip it slowly. With each sip, feel Flora's creative energy flowing into you, empowering you to attract good things.
6. Refrigerate the potion and drink a little each day, finishing on April 30.

*"At last came the golden month of the wild folk—
honey-sweet May, when the birds come back, and
the flowers come out, and the air is full of the
sunrise scents and songs of the dawning year."*

—Samuel Scoville Jr., American author, naturalist, and lawyer, *Wild Folk*

MAY

Sweet, succulent, and beautiful beyond belief, nature unwraps her abundant charms this month and displays them unabashedly for us to enjoy. Likewise, the gorgeous goddesses of May—Maeve, Pachamama, Bast, Seshat, and Iris—invite us to throw off inhibitions and celebrate life. In this section you'll meet these deities and share in their adventures. They'll show you how to live life to the fullest, to revel in the richness of the season, and to make the most of the gifts you've been given. Under the guidance of May's muses, you'll learn to appreciate yourself and value your abilities.

MAEVE

DATES FOR INVITING HER: *May 1–7*

Irish legends say that in early May the fairies emerge from their winter burrows and embrace spring with singing, dancing, and feasting. On May 1,
the Celtic fertility holiday Beltane is celebrated, and traditionally sex plays
a part in the festivities. Therefore, we honor the lusty goddess Maeve, also
known as the Fairy Queen, during this week.

HERSTORY

Also called Medb, this strong-willed, independent Irish goddess is a powerful deity indeed, and a glamorous one. She alone determined which men
would become kings. Legend says no male, human or divine, could look
at her without succumbing to the throes of passion. Not only did Maeve
employ her irresistible beauty to seduce Ireland's kings—discarding them
when she tired of their attention—she also used her sensual power to defeat
the armies of Ulster in battle.

According to one myth, known as the Cattle Raid of Cooley, Maeve and
her consort King Aillil argued about which of them was wealthier. The king
claimed his magic bull made him the richer of the two. The goddess, who
didn't own a magic bull, decided to steal one from a king of Ulster and best

Aillil. Riding in her war chariot, she led a band of soldiers against the Ulster-ites, and she so inflamed them that they fell on the ground, writhing with desire for her. Maeve managed to capture the bull, but the effort was all for naught—it fought King Aillil's bull and both animals died in the process.

Her Animal Totems

The legend of the Cattle Raid of Cooley links Maeve with bulls, which symbolize her characteristics of fertility, strength, and determination, but this goddess has other animal totems as well. According to folklore, magic birds perch on Maeve's shoulders and sing words of wisdom in her ears. Ravens and small animals accompany her too.

Many Irish legends center on Maeve. One says she could run faster than the swiftest horse. According to another, she's the queen of the fair-ies and joins in their merrymaking; she can also take human form if she chooses. Still others give her dominion over the earth and its fruitfulness.

REASONS TO INVITE HER

If you seek to win the heart of a lover—especially if you have a rival—invite Maeve to share her secrets of seduction with you. If you're involved in a conflict with a spouse or partner, such as a divorce or property contest, ask this goddess of love and war to help you gain what's rightfully yours. Invite Maeve when you face a competition that requires courage and self-determination—she'll show you how to trust yourself and your own judgment. This passionate, dynamic, and uninhibited deity can also teach you how to own your power and sexuality, and to express it without reservation.

Symbols and Correspondences

Legends say Maeve had a fondness for gold and other riches. In art and lore, she's often depicted wearing a red dress, perhaps to signify her passionate nature or her role as a warrior deity, and she sometimes brandishes a sword.

HOW TO INVITE HER

Maeve's name means "intoxication" or "she who intoxicates." If you're game, you can make your own honey mead—one of the oldest alcoholic beverages, said to be named for her—to summon the goddess, but it requires some brewing equipment and takes a while to ferment. (You can find recipes and instructions online if you decide to give it a go.) Here's an easier, though less authentic, option that nonetheless will help you embrace your sexuality, connect with your personal power, and trust your own judgment. You'll need:

- *A bottle of dry red wine (or apple cider if you choose not to drink an alcoholic beverage)*
- *A 2-quart pot*
- *A spoon, preferably silver or silver plate*
- *Honey, to taste*
- *Selected fresh fruit, peeled and sliced thin (oranges, cherries, pears, peaches, etc.)*

1. Pour the wine into the pot.
2. Spoon in as much honey as you like.
3. Heat on low for several minutes, while stirring to dissolve the honey and blend it into the wine. Ask Maeve to infuse the wine with her vitality and allure.
4. Add the fruit slices and let the brew simmer just long enough for the fruit to heat and soften, but don't let it get mushy.
5. Allow the wine to cool enough to drink, then serve it in a heat-resistant goblet or cup. Feel the goddess's seductive power flowing into you. If possible, share this goddess-blessed beverage with a lover. Or, envision the lover you seek while you sip the potion.
6. Eat honey cakes or sweet bread as part of this ritual—and make sure to leave some outside for the fairies.

PACHAMAMA

DATES FOR INVITING HER: *May 8–14*

Like many earth goddesses throughout the world, the Inca's Pachamama presided over both planting and harvesting the crops. This time of the year marks the end of the harvest in the Andes, when the last of the crops have been brought in and her people thank Pachamama for her gifts of abundance and well-being. She's also honored during the month of August, which is winter in the Andes, with a ritual called Challa that prepares the land for the planting season.

HERSTORY

The Inca understood the importance of Pachamama to their survival. During the planting season, women sprinkled cornmeal (maize) in their terraced, mountainous fields to thank the deity for her blessings in the past and to request her continued assistance for a bountiful harvest in the future. They also buried food as offerings to the goddess.

Early legends sometimes describe this goddess as cruel and demanding, but usually she's portrayed as calm, peace-loving, and benevolent. If she felt disrespected, however, she shivered and her movement caused earthquakes. But although the goddess could bring destruction when she chose to—she's a wild,

primal force of nature, after all—Pachamama generally personifies the kind and generous mother deity who takes care of her earthly children, protects them, and shares her bounty with them. She's synonymous with Mother Earth, Mother Nature, and the mother of everything on the planet—her name means "mother of all." The mountain peaks represented her breasts and the rivers her milk, which provided nourishment to her people. Sometimes she's depicted as half-woman, half-mountain.

Her Animal Totems

Some legends say Pachamama lived in Peru's Andes Mountains, where she took the form of a dragon.

We often connect Pachamama with Peru and Machu Picchu, but the Incan Empire once stretched through the Andes from Colombia to Chile, until the Spanish invaded and devastated the indigenous population. Even though the original Incan Empire no longer exists, people in the Andes Mountains still honor the goddess today. And, as their ancestors did, her modern-day followers seek her blessings by offering gifts of food and drink to Pachamama. Her devotees prepare special ritual meals and serve the goddess first. They also sprinkle a fermented beverage called chicha on the ground for the goddess and toast her before drinking themselves. In this way, they recognize Pachamama as the guest of honor and the source of continued good fortune.

REASONS TO INVITE HER

Are you working hard to grow a business? Putting energy and imagination into fulfilling an artistic goal? Do you have an idea you want to bring to fruition? If so, ask Pachamama to nourish your endeavor with her creative power and help you manifest your dream. She can teach you how to attract abundance of all kinds, how to enjoy and share your riches, and how to prosper in your chosen field. By bringing you into balance with the earth, the goddess also enables you to draw upon nature's life-restoring power, and to appreciate your connection with Mother Earth.

> ### Symbols and Correspondences
> At festivals to Pachamama, devotees offer her some of her favorite things: fruit, candy, nuts, corn, potatoes, cigars, coca leaves, daisies, beer, and wine.

HOW TO INVITE HER

The people of Sucre, Bolivia, celebrate Pachamama with parades, barbecues, and other festivities. You can enact this version of a good luck ritual to the goddess to attract abundance in many forms. As part of the celebration, you may wish to cook a ritual meal and share it with friends and loved ones. You'll need:

- *A barbecue grill, hibachi, cauldron, or fireplace*
- *Firewood (unless you're using a gas-fired grill)*
- *Matches or a lighter*
- *Incense*
- *A small block of wood*
- *Chicha or beer*
- *Brazil nuts*

1. Build a fire in the barbecue grill, hibachi, cauldron, or fireplace.
2. Light sticks of incense and position them at the corners of the grill or toss loose incense in the fire.

3. Place the block of wood, which represents abundance, in the fire.

4. Sprinkle a little beer at each corner of the grill to chase away unwanted spirits or energies.

5. Pour some of the beer on the ground as an offering to Pachamama.

6. Toast the goddess, and then drink the remainder of the beer yourself.

7. Sprinkle some nuts on the ground for Pachamama and toss a few in the fire, then eat some yourself (unless you're allergic to nuts, of course).

8. Offer prayers to the goddess and ask her to use her powers of fertility to increase your prosperity.

9. If you wish, you can now cook a ritual meal to celebrate—lamb stew with garbanzo or fava beans, corn, potatoes, and cabbage is traditional in some places. Remember to serve Pachamama first!

BAST

DATES FOR INVITING HER: *May 15–21*

We honor the beloved cat goddess Bast (also known as Bastet) this week. The ancient Egyptians celebrated her in April and May, in the city of Bubastis—her annual festival is said to have attracted more than 700,000 revelers. Bast was, and still is, one of the most popular Egyptian goddesses, second only to Isis (July 10–16).

HERSTORY

Early legends and art depict Bast as a lioness or a woman with the head of a lioness. Over time, however, her fierce nature softened, her temperament became more playful, and her image shifted to that of a domestic cat. Like our feline friends today, she personifies grace, beauty, and independence.

Friends and Foes

Bast was closely connected to the ferocious lion-headed Egyptian goddess Sekhmet (July 24–30)—by some accounts they shared a husband—and both were revered as protector deities who punished transgressors. Both bear similarities to their predecessor, Mafdet, the first feline deity in Egyptian history, who was also considered a goddess of justice and a protector deity who killed poisonous snakes.

Not only did Bast provide protection in the home; she also accompanied the souls of the deceased into the afterlife. When royalty and other notables died, they had their favorite felines mummified and placed in their tombs to join them in the next world. Visitors to Bast's festivals at Bubastis brought the bodies of their dead cats with them to be buried in her city, and her devotees kept cats as honored companions.

The early Egyptians considered cats sacred. According to ancient writings, people who killed cats were believed to be responsible for inflicting plagues on humankind. In return for the care and respect people lavished on Bast's earthly counterparts, the goddess served as a divine defender and arbiter of justice—and woe be to those who harmed not only cats but also innocent individuals, especially women and children.

Symbols and Correspondences

Legends link Bast with perfume and aromatic ointments. Some people theorize that her name means "she of the ointment jar," perhaps connecting her with healing salves; her son Nefertum was the god of aromatherapy. She also loves jewelry and is often shown wearing earrings and a collar-like necklace called a menat.

REASONS TO INVITE HER

A playful, fun-loving goddess, Bast encourages you to let go of your inhibitions and fears, and to enjoy life. She's considered the goddess of song and dance—let her show you how to express yourself and find pleasure through music and movement. The Egyptians also revered her as a protector deity who guarded women and children against illnesses (perhaps by killing rodents that carried diseases), so you can call on Bast to keep you and your loved ones safe from health threats. Cats know how to relax, and if you've been working too hard or feel stressed out, the cat goddess reminds you that rest and play are important too.

HOW TO INVITE HER

Bast's followers celebrated her with singing, dancing, and merrymaking. Many of them traveled by boat to Bubastis, playing rattles known as sistrums, drums, and tambourines along the way. Marked with wine and feasting, her holiday was a joyful and liberating event during which inhibitions were temporarily relaxed. You, too, can invite the goddess as the ancient Egyptians did by following these steps:

1. Anoint yourself with your favorite perfume or essential oil.
2. Don a pretty necklace and earrings, or other jewelry. You may want to wear a charm or other image of a cat.
3. If you're a musician, play upbeat tunes to honor Bast. If you don't consider yourself musically adept, put on a lively song and join in as best you can. Shake a rattle, beat a drum, shake a tambourine, or clap your hands enthusiastically.
4. Dance and sing. Shrug off your inhibitions. Don't worry about how you look or sound, just feel the pleasurable sensation of moving with the music. Sense the goddess dancing beside you. Emulate her flowing, graceful motions; spin, jump, dip, arch your back.
5. When you've danced enough, pour yourself a glass of wine or pomegranate juice and toast Bast. Feel yourself relaxing, opening up, shedding self-restraint and judgment.
6. Ask the goddess to bring you happiness and good health, then drink the wine or juice.
7. If you have a cat companion, give it extra attention and some treats this week.

SESHAT

DATES FOR INVITING HER: *May 22–28*

This week, while the sun is in Gemini—the sign astrologers connect with literature, writing, and communication—we honor the Egyptian goddess Seshat. She's the divine patroness of librarians in a country that once was home to the renowned Library of Alexandria, the central repository of the world's knowledge.

HERSTORY

The daughter of the sky goddess Nut (February 19–25) and the earth god Geb, Seshat is the sister of the better-known Egyptian deities Isis (July 10–16), Osiris, Nephthys (November 13–19), and Seth. She oversaw the library of the ibis-headed god Thoth, who governed knowledge and is often credited with inventing writing. However, it's quite likely that Seshat, his consort, actually developed writing/hieroglyphics and Thoth got the accolades. At the time, writing wasn't merely a way of keeping track of data—it was a sacred art, a form of magic that brought conditions into being.

Seshat means "female scribe," and in her role as the Mistress of the House of Books, she took care of the scrolls that contained historical information, financial accounts, science and mathematics, medical knowledge, and the secrets of magic. Additionally, according to myth, this deity stored a copy of each book written on earth in a heavenly library. She kept records of the pharaohs' activities, their governance of Egypt, wars with other nations and the booty captured, matters pertaining to lineage, taxes paid and due, economics, and so on. The goddess even used her understanding of astrology to determine how long each pharaoh would live. Sometimes she's depicted wearing a headdress with a seven-pointed star and crescent on it, perhaps indicating her expertise in astrology and astronomy, which she used to track cycles in Egypt's destiny.

Symbols and Correspondences

It's no surprise that this goddess of knowledge and learning would highly prize books. She also valued ancient tools that, in early Egypt, aided human beings' technical abilities, much as our computers do today. These included the abacus (a device for doing mathematical calculations) and the astrolabe (a tool that charted planetary movements in relationship to the earth).

In addition to creating the written word, the multitalented Seshat taught humankind other valuable skills, including astronomy, architecture, and geometry. Her knowledge of building made her the patroness of carpenters, masons, and other craftsmen who work with their hands (interestingly, astrology links the hands with the sign Gemini). Seshat also kept a census, logging the births, deeds, and deaths of ordinary citizens as well as the rulers and divinities.

Friends and Foes

Because Seshat was responsible for tracking the stories of people's lives and deaths, she's sometimes shown assisting her sister Nephthys (November 13–19), goddess of death and mourning. The two deities worked together to prepare the souls of the deceased for their meetings with Ma'at (October 23–29) and Osiris, and to help them on their journey to the afterlife.

REASONS TO INVITE HER

Do you need help finding the right words for your novel, term paper, or business proposal? Ask Seshat for inspiration and direction. She can also guide you in conveying information to other people, whether you're teaching a class, meeting with clients or colleagues, or delivering a speech. This wise and literate goddess can assist you in learning a new subject or skill. She'll even teach you how to attract something you desire by writing it into being. As the ancient Egyptians knew, writing is a form of magic that combines thought and emotion to produce an outcome.

HOW TO INVITE HER

This week, enlist Seshat's aid to manifest an objective in the physical world. Words have great power, which is why people use affirmations, incantations, and chants to generate results. Follow these steps to summon the guidance of Seshat:

1. Choose a time and place where you won't be disturbed, and can devote yourself to your endeavor.
2. Begin writing a story that describes your situation and intention. Put yourself at the center of the activity. Don't worry about your literary ability and don't censor yourself.
3. Engage your emotions. Envision the action and characters vividly. However, you needn't include every little detail of what will happen—it's actually better to let Seshat and the universe take care of some things. Your story can be short or long, but it should have a happy ending—the outcome you seek.
4. When you've finished, thank Seshat for guiding you and trust the result will be right for you.

IRIS

DATES FOR INVITING HER: *May 29–June 4*

In Greek mythology, Iris is a divine messenger. Therefore, during this second week of Gemini—which astrologers consider the sign of communication—we honor this beautiful goddess who not only fostered communication between the Olympians, but also governed the interactions between land, sky, and sea.

Friends and Foes

In addition to her job as cosmic postal worker, Iris served as assistant to the Greeks' top goddess, Hera (October 16–22), wife of Zeus. This divine couple was notorious for their squabbles, and Iris often mediated for them. Artists sometimes show her standing between the two deities and offering them a loving cup to dispel their discord.

HERSTORY

Legends tell us the speedy Iris was kept busy carrying messages back and forth between the deities. Sometimes shown with wings, Iris also flew down from Mount Olympus regularly to let mortals know the wishes of the gods and goddesses, and she brought back news of earthly goings-on to the Olympians. She predates the better-known messenger god Hermes, and according to Homer's epic *Iliad*, only Iris was trusted to convey information from Zeus.

The ancients knew Iris as the goddess of the rainbow; her name means "rainbow" in Greek. Visually, the rainbow's arc joins heaven and earth, forming a colorful symbol of the connection between the deities and humankind, as well as the goddess's role as liaison between the two realms. The rainbow signifies Iris's parentage too—her mother, Elektra, was a sky/cloud nymph and her father, Thaumas, a sea god. Together, air and water (plus sunshine) create rainbows.

In metaphysics, the elements air and water represent intellect and intuition, respectively, suggesting that Iris uses both forms of communication to share cosmic information with us. This rainbow goddess's association with the elements of air and water also symbolizes the benefits of combining logic and imagination, left and right brain functioning in our everyday lives. By utilizing both, creations born of divine inspiration become possible.

Symbols and Correspondences

Art and legend sometimes depict Iris holding a vessel with which she collects water from earth's rivers and seas, and then brings it back to the heavens to refill the rain clouds. She also appears holding a caduceus, a symbolic winged staff, which in early Greece stood for trade, transferring knowledge, and negotiation.

REASONS TO INVITE HER

Whenever you need to communicate effectively with someone—especially if the usual methods aren't working—ask Iris to convey your message quickly and clearly. Due to her facility in both intellectual and intuitive areas, she can teach you the best way to tap into divine guidance and to share information gleaned from the higher realms. Her experience in dealing with Hera and Zeus has honed her skill in the art of romantic negotiation, so if you've hit a snag in discussions with a lover, invite Iris to smooth the way. She can also help you communicate with the deities and journey into the realm of spirit, where higher knowledge awaits you.

HOW TO INVITE HER

This ritual utilizes the powers of thought and word in creating your physical reality. Before a situation takes form in the material world, it develops in the realm of ideas and imagination. This is the secret behind the Law of Attraction. When you communicate with Iris in this way, she'll gladly assist you in making your wish come true. You'll need:

- *Colored pencils or markers*
- *Paper*
- *An envelope*

1. Think of something you want to happen in your life, then choose a pencil or marker of a color that represents your objective: pink for love, gold for prosperity, blue for serenity, green for healing or growth, etc.
2. On the paper, write a letter to Iris asking her to help you create the result you desire. State your intention in a positive way; for example, "Please bring me good health" not "Keep me from getting sick."
3. While you write, envision the outcome you seek, as if it already exists for you.
4. When you've finished, read the letter aloud to Iris and thank her in advance for her assistance.
5. Fold the letter and slip it into the envelope. Draw a rainbow on the envelope.
6. Sleep with the letter under your pillow at night, until your wish comes true.

"It was June, and the world smelled of roses. The sunshine was like powdered gold over the grassy hillside."

—Maud Hart Lovelace, American author, *Betsy-Tacy and Tib*

JUNE

As we move through late spring and into summer, the golden days of June unfold in a blaze of beauty. Like the earth at this time of the year, the goddesses Benzaiten, Tara, Fortuna, and Hathor offer us their gifts of pleasure and fruitfulness. These goddesses share their stories with you in this section. They'll help you appreciate the wonders around you and encourage you to express your own wonderfulness. Love, they remind us, makes the world go 'round, and the more you give the more you get.

BENZAITEN

DATES FOR INVITING HER: *June 5–11*

This week we honor the Japanese goddess Benzaiten. Like many spring goddesses, she personifies love, creativity, and beauty. Myths connect her with knowledge, music, art, and the good fortune that spring, in its fullness, promises. The Japanese also celebrate her on New Year's Day.

HERSTORY

Benzaiten's roots lie in Hindu tradition, but she's revered in the Buddhist and Shinto religions as well. Also known as Benten, she came to Japan somewhere around the sixth century and promptly took her place of honor as the only goddess among the male-dominated Seven Gods of Good Fortune, or Shichi Fukujin, aboard their Treasure Ship (*Takarabune*). So beloved is she that legend says the island of Enoshima emerged from the sea for the sole purpose of honoring her and giving her a place on earth to stand.

The ancients considered Benzaiten a water goddess, but over time her dominion expanded and her popularity grew. In addition to providing inspiration to artists and musicians, this wise goddess protects children and brings good luck to her followers. She also serves as patroness to Japan's geishas, teaching them grace, knowledge, seduction, and the arts.

Her Animal Totems

Legends connect Benzaiten with dragons—she's often shown riding one—as well as snakes, which she employs as her special messengers. In Japan, dragons are seen as guardians who symbolize power, wisdom, and prosperity. Benzaiten can even turn herself into one of these reptilian creatures when she wants to. According to myth, she tamed a wicked and destructive dragon by marrying him, transforming him with her goodness.

Additionally, she's a favorite goddess of prosperity among the wealthy business and educated classes. As one of the Seven Gods of Good Fortune, her name had the power to attract blessings. Writing one's intentions was considered a magical act, and if a person wrote down his or her monetary objectives, Benzaiten could aid that person in gaining riches.

With all these responsibilities, it's a good thing Benzaiten has many arms—sometimes as many as eight—to handle them all. Usually artists render her holding a *biwa* (a type of mandolin or lute), a spear, a key, a bow and arrow, and a wheel. Two of her hands are pressed together in prayer.

REASONS TO INVITE HER

Are you an artist or musician? Ask Benzaiten to inspire you to expand your talents and reach greater heights. If you seek knowledge or are embarking on a new course of study, this goddess will share her wisdom with you—she's fond of students and truth seekers. She can teach you to make the most of your abilities and to project an image of beauty, grace, and sophistication. She'll guide you in the process of sharing your gifts with the world. If you're searching for love, she can assist you in finding the right partner. Her creative powers can also bring good fortune and happiness in any endeavor—no wonder she's so popular!

HOW TO INVITE HER

This potion infused with goddess energy can help you attract good fortune, especially if you seek prosperity, love, or creative success. You'll need:

- *A tea bag or loose tea leaves*
- *Spring water*
- *A clear glass or plain white cup*
- *A pearl or piece of tumbled jade*
- *A picture of Benzaiten*

1. Brew the tea with the spring water and allow it to cool.
2. Pour the tea into the glass or cup.
3. Drop the pearl or piece of jade into the tea.
4. Lay the picture of Benzaiten on a table, face up, and set the glass or cup on it. Let the glass or cup sit overnight to absorb the goddess's positive energy.
5. In the morning, remove the pearl or jade and drink the tea. Feel Benzaiten's power flowing into you, filling you with her blessings.
6. Sleep with the picture of Benzaiten under your pillow for luck.
7. Carry the gemstone in your pocket or purse to attract good fortune.

TARA

DATES FOR INVITING HER: *June 12–18*

Usually shown as a beautiful young woman, the goddess Tara is one of the most important and revered of the Hindu deities. During this beautiful time of the year, we honor this goddess who, among her many variations, symbolizes the hope of springtime as well as the abundance and fertility of summer.

HERSTORY

The beloved mother goddess Tara is worshipped by not only Hindus but also Buddhists throughout southeastern Asia, Tibet, and Nepal. Her name means "star," a universal symbol of hope, and also "crossing," which signifies her ability to aid humans as they cross into the afterlife. This compassionate deity demonstrates infinite kindness for all beings and shows the way to escape the suffering of physical existence.

A number of legends exist about Tara's origins. According to one, she was once a gentle and generous princess, the essence of goodness and piety. She chose to devote herself to guiding humankind to enlightenment, in order to eventually end the karmic cycle of life, death, and reincarnation on earth. Another story says she emerged from the tears of the enlightened being Avalokitesvara as he wept at seeing the pain mortals endured.

Mythology tells us the goddess presents herself in twenty-one ways, or emanations, which show her myriad natures, powers, and functions. The different colors in which she appears—white, green, blue, and more—symbolize her many roles. Thus, she combines the diverse characteristics and virtues of the feminine principle.

As White Tara, this goddess is the all-seeing divine mother; she has seven eyes and personifies the qualities of pure love, wisdom, and peace. She also possesses healing power and promotes longevity. Artists paint her with smooth white skin, wearing white garments and rich jewels, and holding a white lotus blossom.

Green Tara represents the youthful aspect of the goddess, active and vital, with green skin, splendid jewelry, and holding blue lotuses. In this emanation, she's also a protector deity and savior who brings freedom to her followers by removing obstacles, fears, and attachments.

As Blue Tara, she reminds us of the wrathful destroyer goddess Kali who thwarts her devotees' enemies with her ferociousness. She's also portrayed in numerous other forms, including yellow or gold, which are associated with wealth; red, related to love and passion; and black, indicating power. Sometimes she has two arms, sometimes four, sometimes more. The objects she holds in her hands depict her many facets and responsibilities.

Friends and Foes

Myths connect Tara with several other goddesses, including Parvati (August 28–September 3), Saraswati (February 5–11), and Kali (November 6–12). Each is an individual expression of the Divine Feminine, or Devi.

REASONS TO INVITE HER

Tara has many faces in Hindu and Buddhist mythology, symbolized by the different colors of her skin. If you seek forgiveness or compassion, White Tara will shower you with unconditional love. If you feel a need for safety, Green Tara offers protection and guidance. She'll also give you a little push when you need to take action. Yellow Tara can help you attract prosperity. Blue Tara shows you how to stand up to adversaries courageously.

HOW TO INVITE HER

Each day this week, choose a different version of Tara and get to know her better. In addition to the information offered here, you'll find plenty of online sites that describe the mythology, history, traditions, and beliefs surrounding this goddess. For this ritual you'll need:

- *A multicolored tablecloth, preferably one made in India*
- *Candles in colors that correspond to the colors of the Taras you've chosen to honor*
- *A candleholder*
- *Matches or a lighter*
- *Colorful images of each of the different Taras you've chosen to honor (you can find these online)*
- *Gemstones in colors that correspond to the colors of the Taras you've chosen to honor*

1. Spread the tablecloth on your table.
2. Fit a candle of the appropriate color into the candleholder and light it.
3. Lay one picture of Tara near the candle and set a gemstone of the corresponding color on the picture, as an offering to the goddess.
4. Ask the goddess for assistance in an area related to her powers and attributes. Sense her willingness to help.
5. Commune with her for as long as you like, then extinguish the candle.
6. Repeat each day, focusing on a different aspect of Tara.

FORTUNA

DATES FOR INVITING HER: *June 19–25*

The ancient Romans dedicated temples to Fortuna, the goddess of good luck and prosperity, on June 24, and celebrated her holiday with revelry. Her most significant and elegant temple, the Sanctuary of Fortuna Primigenia, stood in the old town of Praeneste about twenty miles east of Rome. This week we, too, honor Fortuna and seek her blessings.

HERSTORY

The daughter of the top god Jupiter, Fortuna occupies a lofty position in the Roman pantheon. She held the fortunes of individuals and of the nation in her hands and is connected with fate as well as luck. She determined the outcomes of battles, the health and well-being of Rome's citizens, and the success of the emperor, which made her a protector deity too. In early agrarian societies, where a bountiful harvest brought prosperity, she was also seen as a fertility goddess.

Friends and Foes

Fortuna sometimes appears In association with Felicitas, the Roman goddess of happiness and increase, and with Spes, the goddess of hope.

Understandably one of the most popular goddesses among the ancient Romans, Fortuna often appears in art and myth holding a cornucopia, signifying the abundance she bestows on her followers. She's sometimes depicted with a wheel that represents life's cycles and the ups and downs that befall humankind, suggesting that she's unpredictable. Her wheel still shows up today in tarot decks as a card called the Wheel of Fortune, which suggests improved conditions, and as a point in an astrological chart associated with good luck, known as the Part of Fortune.

Naturally, this goddess of fate possessed the skill of divination. A type of fortune-telling event was held at her temple at Praeneste, during which a child selected a wooden rod from many on which possibilities were written. The rod chosen foretold what would occur in the coming year. However, Fortuna is sometimes depicted as blindfolded or veiled to remind us that the future doesn't always reveal itself.

Where to Seek Her

Ideally, you'd want to travel to Rome—or better yet, to Palestrina (formerly Praeneste)—to commune with the goddess, but for most of us that's not possible. Instead, you can find her presiding over fields rich with healthy crops, groves of trees heavy with ripe fruit, and other places that reveal nature's bounty.

REASONS TO INVITE HER

Call on Fortuna to help you attract abundance of all kinds, but especially in financial areas. This may mean a raise, promotion, or return on an investment. This goddess is a favorite among gamblers as well, and she may bring good luck in games of chance or offer a stock market tip. If you've been in a slump lately, ask Fortuna to turn matters around. She can also show you how to protect what's yours. Some sources say Fortuna only bestows her favor on people who've earned it through upstanding moral character and good deeds. Consequently, you may want to keep this in mind as you petition her for aid.

HOW TO INVITE HER

This good luck charm draws on Fortuna's powers through the imagery of the Wheel of Fortune tarot card to attract prosperity. You'll need:

- *An image of The Wheel of Fortune card (download one from the Internet, instead of taking the card from a deck you use)*
- *A pen or marker*
- *A $1 bill (or other currency)*
- *Transparent adhesive tape*
- *A gold- or silver-colored pouch, box, or other container*
- *Dried mint leaves (to attract money)*
- *Dried dill (for good fortune)*
- *Dried parsley (to encourage success)*
- *Ground cinnamon (to speed results)*

1. On the face of the tarot card image write your intention to attract prosperity, stating your request in a positive way, such as "I now have more than enough money for everything I need and want."
2. Hold the $1 bill against the back of the card image and tape the two together.
3. Slip the card and bill into the pouch, box, or other container (fold if necessary).
4. Sprinkle the herbs into the pouch, box, or other container, and close it.
5. Ask Fortuna to assist you in fulfilling your desire.
6. Place this good luck charm on your desk, in your cash drawer, or in a spot where you'll see it often. Or, carry it in your purse or pocket. If you know feng shui, put it in the Wealth Gua of your home—when you stand at your front door looking in, it's the far left section.

HATHOR

DATES FOR INVITING HER: *June 26–July 2*

The Egyptian goddess of happiness, Hathor is the personification of fulfillment—she embodies love, joy, creativity, and all things that make life worth living. Therefore, we honor her now in the fullness of summer, the season of abundance and ease.

HERSTORY

If there's such a thing as a woman's woman, Hathor would be it. As a representative of the feminine force, she's linked in myth with beauty, fertility, and motherhood. This pleasure-loving goddess knows how to have a good time too, and enjoys music and dancing.

The ancient Egyptians were skilled in the art of aromatherapy and used fragrant oils, gums, and resins for everything from seduction to embalming. Not surprisingly, this goddess of love and beauty likes to anoint herself with aromatics—supposedly she has a special fondness for myrrh, which is still prized today for its healing properties. Images of Hathor show her with elaborate eye makeup, perhaps a combination of crushed malachite that Egyptian women used to prevent infections and kohl that protects the eyes from the sun's glare.

But Hathor is also charged with an awesome responsibility: aiding women in childbirth and guarding newborns as they emerge into this world. According to legend, she serves as a cosmic midwife and brings along to each infant's birth a divine support team known as the Seven Hathors, who provide protection to mothers and babes. She even foretells each child's fate. But Hathor doesn't only offer blessings to women on earth; she also oversees their passage into the afterlife where, according to the *Book of the Dead*, they can live on as followers of the goddess.

Her Animal Totems

Because of her maternal nature, legends associate Hathor with the cow goddess Mehet-Weret. Hathor often appears wearing a headdress with two curved horns that hold the sun between them.

REASONS TO INVITE HER

Have you forgotten what it means to be truly joyful? To revel in happiness and to actualize your creative potential? If so, call upon Hathor to help you reconnect with the happiness that is rightfully yours. Ask her to show you how to cast out negative beliefs that erroneously link pleasure with sin. This goddess of protection can also aid expectant mothers through the challenge of childbirth.

Symbols and Correspondences

The lovely Hathor liked to deck herself out in jewelry, especially made of turquoise and malachite, which have been mined in Egypt for thousands of years. Often she's shown wearing a golden menat, a collar-like necklace set with beads that was believed to disperse evil and to engender fertility. It can also be used as a percussion instrument.

HOW TO INVITE HER

If you or someone you know will soon have a baby, enact this ritual to attract Hathor's divine protection and healing. You can also do this to cleanse your living space of unwanted energies, celebrate life, and bring happiness into your home. You'll need:

- *Incense (preferably myrrh or frankincense)*
- *An incense holder*
- *Matches or a lighter*
- *Turquoise and/or malachite gemstones*
- *Egyptian music*
- *A menat, sistrum, or rattle*

1. If you like, don your favorite jewelry and wear colorful eye make-up for this ritual.
2. Fit the incense into the holder and set it on a table or other surface where it can burn safely.
3. Light the incense and invite Hathor to join you.
4. Hold the gemstones in the incense smoke for a few moments to cleanse them, then lay them on the table.
5. Play Egyptian music while you shake the menat, sistrum, or rattle. Dance around the room, shaking the rattle high and low. Feel the heavy, stressful, or unpleasant vibes dispersing and joyful, uplifting energies filling the space.
6. Pick up the incense holder and carry it from room to room, letting the smoke purify your home.
7. Continue shaking the rattle in each room, breaking up stagnant energy and replacing it with good vibes.
8. When you've finished, place the gemstones in the baby's room (if you're performing this ritual for a newborn) or in your own bedroom to provide ongoing protection, health, and happiness.

"Summer afternoon—summer afternoon...
the two most beautiful words in the English language."

—Henry James, American author, *An International Episode*

JULY

At the height of summer, Danu, Isis, Amaterasu, Sekhmet, and Aine—goddesses who radiate like the brilliant July sun—personify the earth's creativity and abundance. As crops ripen in the fields, our own creative powers now come to fruition and shine. Let these five awesome deities show you how to express your creative talents, enjoy the fruits of your labors, and appreciate your innate power. Now is your time to step into the spotlight.

DANU

DATES FOR INVITING HER: *July 3–9*

We celebrate the Celtic mother goddess Danu this week when the sun is in Cancer, the zodiac sign astrologers connect with motherhood. Danu is the oldest of the Celtic deities, dating back to the time when goddess-based spirituality predominated, before Christianity moved into Ireland and supplanted the old ways.

HERSTORY

Long, long ago, the goddess Danu brought her chosen people—the deities known as the Tuatha Dé Danann—back to reign in Ireland after a period of exile, guiding them with the force of her magical powers. This proud race, whom legend says originally ruled Ireland, had suffered a great diminishment in terms of their power and self-esteem, but with Danu's leadership they recaptured their place of respect in Ireland. There she continued to guide and protect them lovingly, teaching them agriculture and sharing her vast knowledge of healing, art, poetry, and fertility with them. Myths say she birthed their leader, Dagda, and is thus the divine matriarch of this legendary race of deities. *Tuatha Dé Danann* means "children of Danu."

As a creator fertility goddess, Danu blends the two feminine forces, earth and water, and their physical counterparts on our planet. Therefore, she signifies fertility and fruitfulness. Through these elements, she also represents change and movement (water's ebb and flow) as well as the earth's seasons. Her name means "flowing one," and throughout Ireland rivers, streams, and wells—and even Europe's Danube—are named for her. The Irish also connect her with sacred stones and sites where her power resides, including the 5,200-year-old passage tomb Newgrange.

REASONS TO INVITE HER

Parents or soon-to-be parents can summon this mother goddess to assist them in the challenges of child-rearing. Danu will lend you her wisdom, guidance, and protection. She can also teach you how to love and care for the members of your family—even the difficult ones—and, by extension, the human family to which we all belong. This week is also a good time to nurture yourself and your inner child. Shower yourself with the TLC you give to others. Let the "flowing one" wash away old hurts, fears, and outdated ideas that may be standing in the way of your happiness.

HOW TO INVITE HER

As children, all of us suffered criticism, loss, anxiety, and other traumas that may have left wounds that still ache today. This meditation connects you with Danu and opens your heart to receive her nurturing and healing love.

1. Sit in a comfortable place where you won't be disturbed. Turn off your phone, TV, and other distractions.
2. Close your eyes and begin breathing slowly and deeply.
3. Imagine you are a child and you are sitting beside a beautiful stream. The goddess Danu is sitting next to you, and you feel safe and happy in her presence.
4. Now recall a time during your childhood when you felt sad, afraid, shamed, or hurt in some way. Allow the emotions from that time to slowly bubble up from within you.
5. Feel the goddess take you in her arms and embrace you. She invites you to climb into her lap, where she holds you and rocks you gently.
6. Wrap your arms around yourself as Danu promises she'll take care of you.
7. Continue hugging yourself as the goddess's love flows into you. Feel the pain easing as you keep breathing slowly and deeply.
8. Hear the peaceful rippling of the stream and sense it washing away the old unhappiness that no longer serves you. Feel yourself growing calmer, stronger, and more joyful.
9. Do this for as long as you wish. When you're ready, thank Danu and open your eyes.

ISIS

DATES FOR INVITING HER: *July 10–16*

Thousands of years ago, the ancient Egyptians honored the goddess Isis and her husband, Osiris, at the festival of Opet. This holiday recognized the revival of Osiris after his death and celebrated the Nile River's annual flooding—thus it marked a time of rejuvenation, renewal, and rebirth. This week, we, too, honor Isis as one of the most important members of the Egyptian pantheon.

HERSTORY

The best-known story of Isis tells us the goddess's brother Set was jealous of the power her husband, Osiris (who was also Set's brother), held in Egypt, and so he murdered him. If that wasn't awful enough, Set cut Osiris's body up into fourteen pieces and scattered them all around Egypt in order to prevent a proper burial.

Isis, however, wouldn't give up. With the help of her sister Nephthys (November 13–19), she scoured the country until she'd collected all of Osiris's body parts—except one, his penis. Using her magical skills she fashioned a temporary wax penis and managed to revive Osiris long enough for him to impregnate her with their son, the powerful god Horus.

Isis's role in Egyptian mythology extends beyond her familial circumstances. She's also considered a protector deity who guarded the pharaohs—early artists depicted her as a mother goddess nursing Egypt's rulers. Furthermore, she guided the souls of the deceased into the afterlife; her magnificent wings offered protection to those making this heavenly journey. Thus, Isis stands as a symbol of everlasting life and of love's power over evil.

Her Animal Totems

Legends tell us the cow was sacred to Isis, as were the scorpion and the snake. She's also shown with hawks, doves, swallows, and vultures—even with a vulture lying on the top of her head. She's most frequently pictured with great wings spread wide to shelter her people.

REASONS TO INVITE HER

Best-known for her devotion to her husband, the god Osiris, Isis can help you respect the sacred nature of a primary partnership. If commitment is a problem for you or your mate, ask Isis to help you learn to trust and value the bond between the two of you, without sacrificing yourself. If you feel you're giving over too much of your power to your partner, or that your family members are critical of your relationship, draw upon Isis's courage to stand your ground. The bravery and determination she displayed after Osiris's murder can offer strength to widows who are grieving the loss of their mates. The goddess assures you that love never dies and your loved ones are safe in the afterlife.

Symbols and Correspondences

Images of Isis often show her holding an ankh, a symbol of eternal life, which suggests her participation in the cycle of life, death, and rebirth. The hieroglyph has been interpreted in many other ways, including as a representation of the union of male and female energies—the circular portion signifies the vagina, the cross below it the phallus.

HOW TO INVITE HER

This week you can mark the goddess's holiday and bring light into the darkness. According to some sources, the ancient Egyptians placed oil lamps on tombs to help the souls of the deceased find their way to the afterlife.

(Note: Use commonsense precautions when lighting candles and lanterns, making sure to burn them in a safe place, in fireproof holders, away from curtains, furnishings, and other flammables. Don't leave burning candles unattended.)

1. Invite friends to join you in a lighted parade through your neighborhood. Ideally, you'll want to carry hurricane or other oil-burning lamps or lanterns in honor of Isis (if you feel that's safe to do). Light each one off the others, passing the light along, to symbolize your connectedness. If using oil-burning lamps is not practical or possible, carry battery-operated flameless pillar candles, glow sticks, or other luminaries.

2. Download Egyptian music to your cell phones and play it as you stroll through the streets.

3. When you've completed your circuit, go to a nearby cemetery or a place where loved ones are buried. If you prefer, go to a spot a loved one considered special or sacred.

4. Place battery-operated candles on the graves to illuminate the souls' way to the afterlife and guide the deceased on their journey.

AMATERASU

DATES FOR INVITING HER: *July 17–23*

We honor the Japanese goddess Amaterasu during the third week of July, when the sun shines brightly in the summer sky (in the Northern Hemisphere). Amaterasu is known as the goddess of the sun, and she's associated with beauty and creativity.

HERSTORY

Like the Greek goddess Athena (January 22–28), Amaterasu had a peculiar birth—she emerged from her father's eye, rather than entering the world in the usual manner. Known for her radiant beauty and goodness, Amaterasu personifies the sun whose light and warmth support all life on earth. From her lofty position, she rules the sky and, by extension, all things that blossom beneath her golden rays. Her important position makes her the most revered goddess in the Shinto religion. Japanese nobles were believed to be her descendants.

The best-known myth about Amaterasu may be based on an actual meteorological event, like the volcanic eruption in C.E. 536 that produced a fog that blocked the sun for eighteen months in many parts of the Northern Hemisphere. Legend explains that Amaterasu had a mean-spirited brother, the storm god Susanoo, who cruelly killed a sacred horse that belonged to her. When she saw the poor creature, the bereft goddess exiled her brother and hid herself away in a cave, refusing to come out. Darkness descended on the earth. Joy disappeared. Evil ran rampant in her absence.

The desperate gods and goddesses attempted to lure the sun goddess out of hiding by placing a sakaki tree outside the cave and hanging her favorite things—glittering gems, fine garments, and a mirror—on it. The ploy didn't work. Finally, one of the goddesses did a wild, erotic dance that made the other deities laugh so loud Amaterasu couldn't contain her curiosity. When she peeked out, she saw her reflection in the mirror and indulged her vanity. She admired herself just long enough for one of the gods to grab her. Her fellow gods and goddesses repositioned Amaterasu in her place of honor in the sky, where her divine light chased away the darkness and troubles on earth. Life returned to normal; goodness and harmony prevailed.

Symbols and Correspondences

Legend tells us the luxury-loving Amaterasu adored jewelry, elegant clothes, and other finery. She's often depicted holding a mirror, her most notable possession. A mirror said to have belonged to the goddess is preserved in her shrine at Ise, where it's ranked as an imperial treasure.

REASONS TO INVITE HER

Amaterasu can teach you to value your own beauty, both inner and outer. Even when you feel sad or hurt or just want to crawl under the covers and hide, this goddess can inspire you to shine your light into the world. We've all suffered losses and injuries, but Amaterasu's radiance illuminates the dark places and brings hope. Let her teach you to laugh again and have fun. She can also show you how to beam a ray of sunshine into other people's lives by drawing upon her generosity and benevolence.

HOW TO INVITE HER

Get in touch with your own beauty and self-worth this week by taking one or more of the following suggestions. Often we're too critical of ourselves and overlook the unique and wondrous qualities that make each of us special. With the guidance and encouragement of Amaterasu, you can learn to value your personal radiance.

1. If possible, go outside and stand in the sunlight for a few minutes each day. Feel Amaterasu's brilliance flowing into you as she shines her divine spotlight on you. If you can't go outside, stand under a bright light.

2. Gaze at your image in a mirror and repeat an affirmation, such as "I am beautiful, lovable, and worthy of all the good things in life. I am a child of the goddess and inherently precious."

3. Each day choose one thing about yourself that you consider beautiful or valuable. It could be a physical feature or a character trait. Spend some time appreciating this special part of yourself.

4. At the end of the week, do something to celebrate your beauty, perhaps by getting a new hairstyle, facial, or pedicure.

SEKHMET

DATES FOR INVITING HER: *July 24–30*

At the height of summer's heat we honor the lion goddess Sekhmet, whom Egyptian myths say created the deserts with her fiery breath. The sun is in Leo this week, the zodiac sign astrologers say is ruled by the sun, and Leo's symbol is the lion. Ancient Egyptians feted the goddess between June and September, the period during which the Nile overflowed and fertilized crops.

Symbols and Correspondences

Sekhmet often holds an ankh, a symbol of life. It indicates the deity's power over life and death and her ability to reawaken the dead in the afterlife. According to some schools of thought, the circular top of the ankh symbolizes the sun, while the cross below it represents the earth.

HERSTORY

Daughter of the Egyptian sun god Ra, Sekhmet is revered as a warrior goddess who accompanied the pharaohs on the battlefield and protected them. Her name means "she who is powerful." Myths and artwork depict her as a fearless lioness or as a woman with the head of a lion. Sometimes she wears a disc as a crown, which represents the scalding sun whose intense summer heat withers the earth.

One legend says Ra gave up on human beings and commanded Sekhmet to kill them all. She embarked on a reign of terror and might have slain everyone on earth if Ra hadn't relented and tricked her. He created a lake of wine, or perhaps of beer stained red with pomegranate juice. When the goddess drank it, thinking it was blood, she got so drunk she couldn't go on.

This ferocious deity not only engages in death and destruction; she's also a divine healer whose priestesses and priests in ancient Egypt were often physicians. Legends say her intimidating nature scared diseases away. But she's also reputed to have inflicted her enemies and those who disrespected her with plagues. Thus, she is a creator and destroyer goddess, a well-known dichotomy in mythology that suggests before something new can be born the old must die. And so, the cycle of life-death-rebirth continues.

Friends and Foes

Myths tell us that Sekhmet had a close alliance with the Egyptian goddess Ma'at (October 23–29) and acted as her protector. Ma'at's job was to decide which deceased souls were worthy to enter the afterlife, and she did this by weighing their hearts on a set of cosmic scales. If a heart weighed in lighter than a feather, Ma'at granted the soul access to the higher realms. If the soul failed the test, another lion deity known as Ammit feasted on the heart.

REASONS TO INVITE HER

At times we all feel weak, frightened, or inadequate to measure up to the demands and challenges life throws at us. During moments of doubt, you can petition the fierce and fearless Sekhmet and ask her to accompany you onto your personal battleground. She'll make you feel more lion-hearted. Is someone contesting you in the career world? Do you fear the powers of a romantic rival? Is a health issue threatening your well-being? If so, Sekhmet can lend you her courage and show you how to face the adversary with strength and self-confidence.

HOW TO INVITE HER

In early rituals to Sekhmet, her devotees performed acts of respect before a different representation of the goddess each day of the year. This week you can engage in an abbreviated version of this age-old practice. You'll need:

- *7 images of Sekhmet (You can download online pictures of the goddess and print them, or you can find artists' illustrations of her in books and scan them. Even better, use figurines of the goddess in this ritual.)*
- *Red wine or pomegranate juice*

1. Position your representations of Sekhmet in a circle, in a place where they can remain throughout this week. If you can't leave them for that long, set them out each day for your ritual and collect them afterward.
2. Each day, stand before one image of Sekhmet and request her assistance in dealing with a challenge you face.
3. Engage in a mental dialogue with the goddess, during which you offer devotion to her and receive guidance from her.
4. When you've finished, toast Sekhmet with a glass of red wine or pomegranate juice to thank her for her support.

AINE

DATES FOR INVITING HER: *July 31–August 6*

The ancient Celts celebrated their beloved goddess Aine on August 1, at the harvest festival Lughnasadh (also known as Lammas). On this day, she's said to have created grain and given it to the Irish people. She's also honored on the summer solstice.

HERSTORY

Aine's name means "bright," "joy," "splendor," and "radiance." Celtic mythology originally linked her with the sun and later the moon. However, she plays many roles in legends, and over time, her associations and responsibilities grew. One of her jobs was to preside over the land, ensuring its fertility. She also protected crops and livestock. Naturally, the agrarian people of early Ireland revered her, for they depended on her benevolence for their very existence. In many cultures, we find goddesses who brought grain to their people—the Greeks' Demeter (September 18–24), for example—and in Irish legends, Aine gets credit for creating this important crop. She did it in a rather unusual way, however—she literally gave birth to wheat as if it were her baby.

Celtic lore also describes Aine as a healer. Some stories say the goddess walked the land, offering healing and solace to all who needed it. Her favorite spot was Lough Gur, a lake in Ireland's County Limerick near her sacred hill Croc Aine, which reputedly contained magical properties. There, people came during the full moon to be cured in the healing waters, much as people around the world still "take the waters" at spas and mineral springs.

Her Animal Totems

On the night of the full moon, the goddess rode horseback with her two sisters, Fenne and Grainne, through sacred land in County Limerick. According to folklore, the red-haired Aine was also a shapeshifter, who could turn herself into the red mare Lair Derg, whom none could catch.

Aine also knew the secrets of sacred sex and shared them with mortal men as well as deities. Some say her liaisons produced a race that blended human blood with that of the fairies, who lived in sidhe, or burrows, in Croc Aine. According to one legend, the goddess married the Irish Earl of Desmond and bore a remarkable son, who may have been the fabled magician Merlin.

REASONS TO INVITE HER

Do you feel in need of nourishment and support, in body, mind, or spirit? Are your heartfelt desires and passionate goals unappreciated by others? Do you long to see your dreams blossom, your efforts bear fruit? If so, ask Aine to shine her radiant light on you and show you how to reap the rewards you're due. She can nurture you during the early, growing stages of development and guide you to the "harvest."

If you're experiencing health problems, Aine can aid you as you connect with nature's curative processes. Purification, awakening the Divine within, and embracing joy can be powerful medicine. This goddess also helps you renew the vitality and sacredness in your relationships with others—especially romantic ones—which can send positive energy rippling through other areas of your life.

HOW TO INVITE HER

As our ancestors did for centuries, you can attract the powers of the goddess to aid you in any endeavor, from inspiring creativity to protection to healing. Enact this ritual to petition Aine's assistance. You'll need:

- *An herbal symbol of your intention, such as red rose petals for love, wheat or rice kernels for fertility, mint leaves for abundance, etc. (Note: It's best to request the goddess's help with only one objective at a time.)*
- *An unbleached muslin bag*
- *Biodegradable string*

1. Place the herbal symbols of your objective in the muslin bag and tie it shut with one end of the string.
2. Hang the bag from a tree by tying the other end of the string to a twig or branch.
3. Say a prayer to Aine and ask her to help manifest your desire.
4. As the weather deteriorates the bag and its ingredients fall to the ground, your request is answered.

> *"This morning, the sun endures past dawn.
> I realise that it is August: the summer's last stand."*
>
> —Sara Baume, English author, *A Line Made by Walking*

AUGUST

August is a time of fullness, when life on earth is bountiful and we reap what we've sown. The glowing goddesses Diana, Oshun, Pele, and Parvati personify this bright and beautiful month. As you meet the deities in this section and learn about the traditions that celebrate them, let their experiences inspire you in matters of self-reliance. How have your efforts brought about (or inhibited) abundance? How can sharing your powers with others benefit all concerned? The goddesses' stories can guide you.

DIANA

DATES FOR INVITING HER: *August 7–13*

The ancient Romans worshipped the goddess Diana at Nemoralia, the Festival of Torches, on August 13. This week we, too, honor the fiercely independent deity who protected animals, women, and slaves, as we seek her protection in our own lives.

HERSTORY

The Roman moon goddess Diana is the daughter of Jupiter and the sister of the sun god Apollo. (The Greeks knew her as Artemis.) Considered a maiden goddess, she's often pictured as a teen or young woman dressed in hunting garb. The free-spirited "animal whisperer" swore never to marry and chose to live in the forest among the woodland creatures that she protected and preferred as companions, instead of engaging in the ongoing dramas of her fellow Roman deities. However, she's also known as the goddess of the hunt and is often depicted carrying a bow with a quiver of arrows slung over her shoulder. Thus she represents the sacred hunt, during which an animal offers itself as a sacrifice and is taken with reverence and gratitude, rather than in meaningless slaughter.

As a moon goddess, Diana is linked with and safeguards women and children, who according to astrology are governed by the moon. Mothers-to-be sought her aid in childbirth, and women who wanted to become pregnant asked the goddess to make them fertile. Because she also helped slaves and people of the lower classes in Roman society, she became—and still remains—one of the most revered deities.

According to one myth, the goddess took a fancy to the great hunter Orion, but her brother Apollo disapproved of the match. Apollo challenged Diana to a shooting contest in which she accidentally killed Orion. The heartbroken moon goddess then turned her beloved into a constellation so she could join him in the night sky, and she positioned his loyal hunting dogs near him for companionship (the constellations Canis Major and Canis Minor).

REASONS TO INVITE HER

Do you feel you've become too reliant on someone else or gotten too entangled in other people's affairs? Is a relationship smothering you? Do you need some time and space to yourself? If so, Diana can show you how to be more independent and to stand up for yourself with confidence. She'll teach you how to care for others without losing yourself in the process. Let her guide you into the "woods" that represent your own inner nature and show you how to reconnect with your natural wildness. Diana can also assist women during pregnancy and help mothers care responsibly for their children without limiting their freedom.

HOW TO INVITE HER

This week summon Diana as her Roman followers did, by celebrating her festival. Honor not only the fullness of the season, but also your own wholeness as a person complete and beautiful within yourself.

1. Wear summer flowers in your hair or hang a garland of blossoms around your neck. If you have a pet dog, decorate its collar with flowers that are safe for dogs.
2. Share bread and seasonal fruit with friends and loved ones, and be sure to leave food out for the wild creatures.
3. When the moon rises high in the night sky, light a torch (or a candle) in the goddess's honor. In ancient times, revelers carried burning torches to Lago di Nemi, a sacred lake south of Rome, and shone their light on the surface of the water where it merged with the moon's reflection. If there's a pond, lake, or other body of water near you, you may choose to do the same. Otherwise, simply light your torch (of any kind) and give thanks to Diana for your blessings.
4. Ask the goddess to protect you throughout the rest of the year.

OSHUN

DATES FOR INVITING HER: *August 14–20*

The Yoruba people of Nigeria celebrate Oshun, the goddess of fertility, in her Sacred Grove near Oshogbo with a two-week festival, usually in July or August. At this time of the year, thousands of people visit the nearly two hundred acres of forest dedicated to her, where shrines and artwork abound. This week we, too, honor this gentle, generous, and beautiful deity and align ourselves with her love and kindness.

Her Animal Totems

As the protector of fish and birds, Oshun cares for all the creatures that live in or frequent the waterways of western Africa. The colorful peacock is one of her sacred birds.

HERSTORY

One of the most benevolent of the world's deities, Oshun showers humanity with love of all kinds, not only romantic but also familial and spiritual. Mythology depicts her as a river goddess, known as the goddess of the sweet (or fresh) waters—the River Oshun in Nigeria is named for her.

Throughout history water has symbolized fertility, abundance, and nourishment as well as healing and purification. Oshun represents all these, and more. Like the Asian goddess Kuan Yin (March 5–11), she pours the waters of life onto the world and blesses humanity with joy, compassion, and fruitfulness. Although her kindness and protection extend to all her followers, she lavishes special care on the poor, sick, and orphans.

As is the case with many fertility goddesses, Oshun governs the productivity of the land. Folklore tells us she taught agriculture to her people and brought them prosperity. According to one legend, she joined forces with other female deities to create the earth when the male gods failed at the task. Oshun also knows the art of divination and can tell the future using cowrie shells, a skill she shared with the other deities (known as orishas).

REASONS TO INVITE HER

If you're seeking a new lover or want to sweeten an existing relationship, ask Oshun to school you in the art of seduction. She'll teach you to appreciate your own beauty, to be comfortable with your sexuality, and to open your heart to love. This fertility goddess can also help those who wish to become pregnant. If you've fallen on hard times financially or would like to be more prosperous, she'll bring her knowledge of agriculture to bear and show you how to plant the seeds that attract abundance. Her healing powers can also ease the discomfort of an illness or injury—she may even suggest hydrotherapy, aromatherapy, or a cleansing regimen. Sit beside a body of running water and listen to her voice guiding you.

Symbols and Correspondences

Myths say this luxury-loving goddess has a fondness for all sorts of girlie things, including gold and amber jewelry, shells, and perfume, which she uses to heighten her sensual allure. Sometimes she appears as a mermaid holding a mirror or a circular fan. This sweet-tempered deity also enjoys sweet foods, especially honey and fruit.

HOW TO INVITE HER

Legends say Oshun had magical powers and a special talent for concocting love spells. Invite her to participate in creating this fragrant love oil with you. You'll need:

- *A piece of pink paper*
- *A pen, pencil, or marker that writes red ink*
- *Scissors*
- *Olive oil*
- *A scallop, clam, or cockle shell*
- *Rose, ylang-ylang, patchouli, or jasmine essential oil (or a combination) (these are the most important oils associated with love)*

1. On the pink paper draw a heart with your red pen, pencil, or marker, and then cut it out.
2. Write your intention on the paper heart, stating the outcome you desire in a positive way, for example, "I now have a lover who's right for me in every way." As you work, envision your wish coming true and sense Oshun helping you to achieve your heart's desire.
3. Pour about a tablespoon of olive oil into the shell, so that the shell is about half-full.
4. Add a few drops of the essential oil(s), then stir the mixture with your finger.
5. Put three dots of oil on the heart.

6. Put a dot of oil on your forehead, heart, and solar plexus, which lies about halfway between the heart and belly button. (Note: Some people are sensitive to essential oils, so you may want to do a test beforehand. If your skin does not tolerate the oil, dip a handkerchief in the oil mixture and hold it near your nose as you touch these body points.)

7. When you've finished, take the shell with the remaining oil to a stream or river. Place the shell in the water as an offering to the goddess to thank her for her assistance.

8. Sleep with the paper heart under your pillow each night this week.

PELE

DATES FOR INVITING HER: *August 21–27*

This week we celebrate Pele, the Hawaiian goddess of fire, lightning, and volcanoes. To the native people of Hawaii, she is one of the most popular and respected deities, for without her their islands wouldn't exist. Her creative power bursts forth with wild exuberance, resulting in the incredible beauty and lushness we associate with this time of the year and with Hawaii.

HERSTORY

Folklore tells us this feisty and passionate goddess came to what's now Hawaii from a mystical place known as Kuaihelani. Forced to leave her homeland after falling in love with her older sister's husband, Pele traveled by canoe to escape her angry sister's revenge. Her journey took her along the entire archipelago, stopping at one island after another on the way. Each time she stopped and tried to build a fire pit, her sister, the ocean goddess Namakaokahai, doused it and Pele had to move on. According to one tale, Pele finally came to Maui and climbed to the top of the volcano Pu'u o Pele— too high up for her sister to reach—and made her home there. Another says she lived atop the Kilauea volcano on the island of Hawaii.

Pele's story describes the geological creation of the Hawaiian islands, which formed when volcanoes burst from the ocean and spewed molten lava that later cooled into land. The conflict between the two sister goddesses symbolizes the explosive nature of hot magma hitting the colder ocean, as well as the opposing forces of fire and water. Some sources also suggest the myth describes the battles that go on between siblings, during which the older children teach the younger ones by putting them through difficult tests.

Friends and Foes

In addition to her sister, the sea goddess Namakaokahai, the tempestuous fire goddess Pele clashed with the snow goddesses who lived on Hawaii's mountains. Legend says their fights created the islands' beautiful flowers.

REASONS TO INVITE HER

Pele is both a creator and a destroyer goddess, and she knows that often destruction must occur before something new can arise in its place. If an obstacle is standing in the way of your success or well-being, Pele can help you eliminate it. If you feel discouraged or stuck in a rut, ask the goddess to spark your desire and imagination. She'll lend you her courage to embrace challenges, stand up to adversaries, or carve out a special place where you can express yourself.

Symbols and Correspondences

Fire, of course, is Pele's element. She's also fond of orchids, plumeria, hibiscus, bird-of-paradise, and other tropical flowers. And, she loves to dance the hula.

HOW TO INVITE HER

In Hawaii, the beautiful lei is a sign of friendship, affection, and harmony. Although leis are typically made of orchids or other native flowers, you can make this special lei of colored paper. It can help you tap Pele's power to eliminate problems that are interfering with your peace and happiness. You'll need:

- *Several sheets of colored paper*
- *Scissors*
- *A pen, pencil, or marker*
- *A needle*
- *Thread*

1. From the colored paper cut a number of flower-shaped discs, as many as you need to make a lei that will slip easily over your head. Each blossom should be about 2–3 inches in diameter. The flowers may all be the same color, such as pink for affection, or a variety of colors that represent your objectives.

2. On the blossoms write your intention(s) in pen, pencil, or marker. You may write something you wish to create or bring into your life, or something you want to get rid of. You may write the same intention on all the flowers, or you may choose to write several different intentions—just make sure your lei is designed either to create or destroy, not both.

3. Thread your needle and stitch the paper flowers together to form a lei that's long enough to fit over your head.

4. When you've finished sewing, tie the ends of the thread together to form a necklace, then put on the lei and wear it for at least an hour. During this time, ask Pele to help you achieve your desire. Sense her presence—you may even notice you feel a bit warmer.

5. If your intention is to attract or create, wear the lei each day of this week for at least an hour while you focus on the outcome you seek. Then display it in a place where you'll see it often. If your intention is to eliminate something, burn the lei at the end of the week while you envision problems or obstacles burning away too.

PARVATI

DATES FOR INVITING HER:
August 28–September 3

In India, Parvati is honored with a three-day festival called Hartalika Teej, which takes place in August or September. The holiday celebrates the union of the goddess with Lord Shiva. During the festival, married women pray for the health and longevity of their husbands; single women ask the goddess for happy marriages. This week we, too, recognize Parvati and seek her blessings.

Symbols and Correspondences

The daughter of Himavan, lord of the majestic Himalayas, Parvati loves mountains and rules from the 22,000-foot-tall Mount Kailash in Tibet. In Sanskrit, her name is a word for mountain. Lotus flowers, too, are precious to her, and she's often depicted sitting on a lotus blossom or holding one in her hand.

HERSTORY

According to Hindu myth, Parvati is the goddess of love, marriage, and fertility. The second wife of Lord Shiva, this compassionate and devoted deity took care of him while he grieved the death of his first wife. Eventually—

after a great deal of effort and self-sacrifice on her part—he fell in love with her and the couple went to live on the holy mountain Kailash, where they're said to spend their time doing yoga, meditating, and engaging in sacred sex.

Known for her gentle nature, nurturing kindness, and patience, Parvati manages to keep Shiva's violent temper in check. She's also a wise counselor with an abundance of inner strength—the perfect complement to her husband, the destroyer/war god. Together they symbolize the interdependence of male and female energies, and thus the divine depiction of traditional marriage. As the goddess of marriage, Parvati is always shown in conjunction with Shiva, never alone.

One of the most revered of the Hindu goddesses, she is an embodiment of Shakti (the feminine aspect of creation). Her power is shown in ten aspects, which are represented by other deities, including Kali (November 6–12) and Tara (June 12–18).

REASONS TO INVITE HER

Parvati's festival week is the perfect time to solicit her favor if you want more joy, peace, or understanding in a romantic relationship. However, you can petition her for assistance anytime love goes awry. She can teach you the value of patience and devotion, without sacrificing your own needs, dignity, or power. If you're seeking a happy, fulfilling partnership, call on the goddess to help you attract the ideal mate.

Where to Seek Her

If you live in the mountains, you'll find it easy to sense Parvati's presence way up in the clouds. Otherwise, go to a high place, even if it's the top of a tall building. Imagine you're in the rarified realm of the goddess and ask her to speak to you.

HOW TO INVITE HER

To connect with the goddess, first engage in the ancient Hindu art of hand painting with *mehndi,* or henna, a reddish plant-based dye. Hindu women create intricate and elaborate designs on their hands and feet with this dye—you can find many beautiful patterns and purchase kits online. However, you may prefer to adorn yourself with symbols and images that have special meaning for you—set your intention before you begin.

1. Apply the henna to your hands and/or feet in any pattern that speaks to you. While applying the dye, keep your mind focused on your intention, and with each brushstroke sense Parvati's presence. Be careful not to get the dye on clothing or other materials. The henna designs will last a week or more.

2. With your painted hands, hold a smooth, egg-shaped stone known as a Shiva lingam. Typically, this stone is a form of brownish jasper native to India and combines both light and dark coloring, but you can find Shiva lingams naturally occurring in many places— perhaps in your own backyard. Look for a stone circled by a band of a contrasting shade or one that's half light and half dark in color. They're also available at gem/mineral shops and online. The elongated shape symbolizes the masculine force and Shiva, while the circle represents the feminine and Parvati. Together they signify the union of male and female, the balance of opposites, and the joining of body and spirit that engenders creativity.

3. Meditate while holding the stone. Give thanks to Parvati for guiding and protecting you, for bringing you abundance, and for helping you achieve your intention.

4. When you've finished, place the stone in a spot where you'll see it often to remind you that the goddess is aiding you and all is well.

*"A harvest is also a legacy, for very
often what you reap is...more than you
consciously know you have sown."*

—Faith Baldwin, American author

SEPTEMBER

September begins the harvest season, during which we gather Mother Earth's bounty and prepare for leaner times ahead. The goddesses Hestia, Aja, Demeter, and Nemesis represent both the earth's generosity and the need to manage resources wisely. As you meet them and read their stories in this section, you'll see how the sacred and the mundane are interwoven. You'll also gain insight into how relationships with our fellow humans, with the natural world, and with ourselves affect our well-being.

HESTIA

DATES FOR INVITING HER: *September 4–10*

This week we honor Hestia, the Greek goddess of the hearth. Her characteristics align with those of the zodiac sign Virgo, where the sun is positioned now. Modest, practical, self-sufficient, and reserved, Hestia concerns herself with the mundane tasks of everyday life and makes them sacred rituals.

Symbols and Correspondences

Hestia's most obvious symbol is fire, which we associate with spirit and the divine spark of creativity. Fire also purifies; therefore it's an apt symbol of Hestia's purity.

HERSTORY

Unlike her more famous siblings Zeus, Hera (October 16–22), Demeter (September 18–24), Poseidon, and Hades, Hestia had no interest in power or prestige. Instead, this gentle goddess chose a quiet existence, living in Zeus's home without a husband or children of her own. According to legend, the gods Apollo and Poseidon loved Hestia, but she worried that if she chose either of them the other would be disappointed and her peace would be destroyed. Not wanting to stir up trouble on Mount Olympus, Hestia vowed to remain a virgin forever. Nevertheless, she presides over home, family, and domestic life.

The goddess's most notable responsibility was tending the hearth, which in ancient Greece served as the domestic and spiritual center of the home. Here families prepared food and people made offerings to the deities—and it was important to keep the fire burning at all times. Therefore the hearth represents Hestia's dual role as nurturer and priestess, the goddess who understands that both the mundane and the divine are essential parts of human existence.

Hestia was also charged with maintaining order within communities, and each municipality had a public hearth where people worshipped her. There her devotees could make offerings to the goddess in return for her protection. When people moved away from a city to establish a new settlement, they took along fire from her communal hearth to light a sacred hearth in their new home. In so doing, they brought the goddess with them too.

Where to Seek Her

You can find Hestia in places where food is prepared and also where you find comfort and camaraderie. She abides in your cook stove, your home's fireplace, and the fire pit where you sit around to share stories with family and friends. Gaze into the flames and see her image smiling back at you.

REASONS TO INVITE HER

As she did in days of old, Hestia can protect your home and family. If you're experiencing tension or upsets in your domestic life, ask this peace-loving deity to help restore order and harmony. Sometimes the serenity you seek comes from finding a holy center and realizing that your everyday existence isn't separate from your spiritual one. Each action can be sacred if you see it that way. Let this goddess show you how to be fully present in your daily tasks and to exercise mindfulness in all you do. Hestia can also show you how to detach from emotional dramas and look at situations from a more practical perspective.

HOW TO INVITE HER

The early Greeks gave offerings to Hestia at the beginning and end of each meal, and always presented her with the choicest portion. This week, you can do the same to attract her favor and bring peace and abundance to your home.

1. If you have a fireplace, woodstove, or barbecue grill, light a special fire to honor Hestia and eat in front of it. Even better, cook your meal over the fire instead of the stove. Legend says you should light the fire by shining sunlight through a glass to kindle a spark, but that's probably not practical today. If you don't have a place to build a fire, light a candle and set it at the center of your table. Or, go to a public park, campground, or other place where you can make a fire safely.

2. Make an offering to the goddess—traditional offerings included fruit, wine, olive oil, and year-old calves—and ask her to join you. Express gratitude for the food you're eating and all those who made it possible: people, animals, plants, the earth.

3. Toast Hestia with red wine or pomegranate juice.

4. Give thanks for the many blessings in your life, small as well as large.

5. After you've finished eating, pour a small amount of wine or juice into the fire, but don't extinguish it—let it burn out naturally. If it's safe to do so, say, in a woodstove, keep the fire going throughout the week.

AJA

DATES FOR INVITING HER: *September 11–17*

This week the sun is in the zodiac sign Virgo, an earth sign astrologers connect with healing and plant-based medicine. Therefore we honor the Yoruba's cosmic herbalist, Aja, at this time.

> ### Symbols and Correspondences
> Legends say Aja created yams, which are an important staple in the diet of the Nigerian people. Nigeria produces more yams than any other country.

HERSTORY

This benevolent Yoruba orisha, or protector goddess, abides in the forests of West Africa where she cares for the animals and plants that live there. Known as the Lady of Forest Herbs, she's the divine environmentalist and a wise woman who understands the inner lives of all earth's creatures. In addition, Aja possesses healing powers and knows the secrets of herbal medicine, which she taught to her followers.

According to folklore, if you want to meet Aja you must allow yourself to get lost in the forest. If you're respectful, she'll share her plant magic with you.

The forest often appears in mythology as a symbol for a shamanic journey. You enter it to discover your inner truth and a world beyond the ordinary, mundane one you usually occupy. A shaman herself, Aja leads you into this hidden realm and puts you in touch with the primal wildness that lies within you. She may also teach you to shapeshift, to take on an animal form temporarily—at least in spirit—in order to gain that animal's powers and knowledge. Some stories say Aja whisks people away in the guise of the "wild wind" to another world, and keeps them there for seven days or longer—they return with special powers.

Where to Seek Her

Although the best place to seek Aja is deep in the forest, you can also find her in any woodland, arboretum, or park. Listen for her voice in the wind as it rustles the leaves of the trees. Observe the plants that live there. Hug a tree or climb it.

Aja's connection with the earth and her ability to make plants grow also links her with fertility and abundance, like the better-known goddesses Demeter (September 18–24) and Gaia.

REASONS TO INVITE HER

If you're interested in learning about herbalism or another plant-based therapy, ask Aja to take you on as her student. If you have an ailment that you'd like to treat with natural remedies, she'll guide you to the healing methods that can ease your distress. She can also show you how to concoct your own lotions, salves, etc. Aja serves as the patroness of gardeners, arborists, and organic farmers, as well as those who seek to live a "green" life. This earth goddess can teach you to exist in harmony with the other life-forms on our planet and realize that you are connected with All That Is. In the process, you'll be nourished in body, mind, and spirit.

HOW TO INVITE HER

Make this soothing herbal tea to ease a stomachache or improve digestion. You can drink it hot or cold. With this simple ritual, you invite the goddess to share her healing herbs and plant wisdom with you. You'll need:

- *A pot or kettle*
- *4 cups of water*
- *A teapot*
- *Chamomile tea, 2 teaspoons of loose leaves or a tea bag*
- *Green tea, 2 teaspoons of loose leaves or a tea bag*
- *Peppermint tea, 2 teaspoons of loose leaves or a tea bag*
- *Fresh ginger, to taste, grated*
- *Honey, to taste*
- *Lemon juice, to taste*
- *A spoon*
- *A teacup or mug*

1. In the pot or kettle, heat the water to boiling. While you're waiting for it to boil, ask Aja to join you and bless you with her healing power. You may want to say a prayer or incantation to her.
2. Pour a little of the hot water into the teapot and swirl it around to warm the pot.
3. Put the tea into the teapot, then pour in the rest of the hot water. Add fresh ginger, honey, and lemon juice to the tea and stir the mixture three times in a clockwise direction.
4. When it's as strong as you want it to be, strain out the tea leaves or remove the tea bags.
5. Pour some tea into the cup or mug if you plan to drink it hot. If you'd rather drink it cold, let it cool to room temperature and then refrigerate.
6. Drink as much as you like and store the rest in the fridge for later. As you sip the tea, feel the goddess granting you her blessing of health.

DEMETER

In many parts of the world September is harvest time, when we reap the earth's bounty in preparation for the darker days that lie ahead. This week we recognize Demeter, one of the oldest and most important of the Greek goddesses, also known as the goddess of grain or the corn goddess. Her ancient festival, Thesmophoria, was usually celebrated in the autumn and only adult women attended. The Mystery rites held in her honor at the town of Eleusis, north of Athens, took place in September.

HERSTORY

The goddess of agriculture in ancient Greece, Demeter held a powerful and prestigious position, for it was she who made the fields fertile and the crops thrive. She also taught human beings how to grow fruit, corn, wheat, and to bake bread. Like many fertility goddesses, she's depicted as a Mother Earth deity who nourishes her people. Artists often show her holding a sheaf of wheat or a cornucopia.

Demeter's maternal devotion is the subject of one of the best-known myths about her. As the story goes, the goddess's only child, a beautiful young daughter named Persephone, was kidnapped by Demeter's brother Hades. This god of the underworld wanted the girl for his wife and dragged her down into his kingdom beneath the earth. Naturally, Demeter was heartbroken and desperately tried to rescue her daughter, but without success. The top god Zeus, brother of both Demeter and Hades, offered no help at all.

Friends and Foes

When Demeter sought help from the gods to force Hades to release her daughter, only the goddess Hecate (October 30–November 5) came to the distraught mother's aid and attempted to negotiate Persephone's freedom. After Persephone and Demeter were reunited, Hecate remained as the girl's companion.

Angry, Demeter decided to force the Olympians' hands. She withdrew her fertility from the earth. Nothing grew. Famine spread across the land. Zeus finally relented and told Hades to let the girl go. There was a problem, however. While imprisoned, Persephone ate some pomegranate seeds, an act that bound her to the god of the underworld. Eventually, the deities worked out a deal. Persephone could spend two-thirds of the year above ground with her mother, but she must live with Hades for the other third: the winter season. As a result of the agreement, Demeter came to govern the seasons, for the land blossomed only while mother and daughter were together. Persephone's descent into the underworld and her return to the realm of the living also represents the cycle of death and rebirth.

REASONS TO INVITE HER

Women who wish to become pregnant can call upon this mother goddess to increase fertility. She can also assist you in raising your children with love, kindness, and patience. Her powers of fertility extend to all creative endeavors in which you seek growth—she'll nurture your efforts at growing a business or fulfilling your artistic talents. If you're a farmer, gardener, or work in the food industry, ask Demeter to be your patroness. Let her perseverance guide you in the pursuit of your goals.

Her Animal Totems

Myths tell us pigs and cattle, which represent fertility, were favorites of the goddess. Some legends also connect her with snakes, symbols of sexuality.

HOW TO INVITE HER

In honor of the grain goddess, bake a loaf of bread and ask her to join you. You may also want to invite a group of your female friends to participate in making and eating the bread. A recipe isn't included here because you should choose a recipe that not only tempts your palate, but is also one that holds a personal symbolic significance for you or whose ingredients represent an outcome you desire. Keep the following in mind as you choose your ingredients:

- *Because Demeter also governed the growth of fruit and fruit-bearing trees, a type of bread that includes fruit may bring you close to the goddess.*
- *Figs and dates are associated with fertility.*
- *Olives are a valuable crop in Greece—a gift from Demeter's fellow Olympian Athena (January 22–28). Consider baking olive bread or basting the loaf with olive oil.*
- *Use fall vegetables, such as squash or pumpkin, in your bread.*
- *If your goal is to attract good luck, put dill in the bread.*
- *Add cinnamon to bring success and prosperity.*
- *Add orange peel to encourage wealth or to bless a business.*
- *If you seek security or advancement in your job, include pecans.*
- *You may also want to serve beer, a beverage brewed from grain, with your homemade bread.*

NEMESIS

DATES FOR INVITING HER:
September 25–October 1

We are now entering the time of the year when we reap what we've sown—not only in terms of harvesting crops but also with regard to our actions in all areas of life. This week, we recognize Nemesis, the Greek goddess of justice and retribution, who shows us where we stand and what we need to work on.

HERSTORY

Today we use the word *nemesis* to mean an opponent, rival, or enemy—and often that person is you, or what psychiatrist C.G. Jung called your "Shadow." In Greek mythology, the goddess by this name forces us to look at ourselves in the mirror and see the truth. She also reminds human beings to honor the deities, and woe be to those who neglect to pay their respects. Nemesis doesn't care how rich or famous you are; she takes all mortals to task and subjects them equally to her authority. Her job is to make sure justice prevails. In fact, she can be especially hard on those who think they're above the law or deserve special treatment.

In a well-known legend, Nemesis punished an insolent young man named Narcissus who treated badly the people who cared for him. In an act of divine retribution, the goddess led him to a reflecting pond—and when he gazed at his image in the water he fell madly in love. Narcissus was so enamored of his good looks that he couldn't pull himself away from the pond; he died there. One story says that upon his death, the narcissus flower came into being.

Although Nemesis may be thought of as a vengeful and ruthless judge, her job is to prevent excesses and unconscionable behavior. Without her, the cruel and powerful would destroy the balance necessary for life on earth to exist.

REASONS TO INVITE HER

Nemesis makes you painfully aware of how you've gotten off track—she reveals your mistakes and points the way back to balance. Ask her to help you put your finances in order, for example, or start an exercise program to get in shape. She insists you take responsibility for your behavior—there's no avoiding this deity, who also goes by the name Adrestia, which means "inescapable."

If someone has wronged you, Nemesis can assist you in bringing about justice. Has a loved one treated you unkindly? A coworker taken credit for your efforts? Are you involved in a legal dispute? The goddess demands the errant person provide restitution, so matters can be resolved justly.

HOW TO INVITE HER

This ritual calls upon the goddess Nemesis to bring justice to a situation in which you feel you've been treated unfairly. It's also designed to let the person who has wronged you see his or her error. You'll need:

- *Sandalwood incense*
- *An incense holder*
- *Matches or a lighter*
- *The Justice card from a tarot deck (you can download this image if you don't have a tarot deck)*
- *An image of the person who has wronged you*
- *A mirror*
- *An image of an old-fashioned scale*
- *Chips of cedar or cedar bark*
- *A fireproof container*

1. Fit the incense into the holder, then set the holder on a table and light the incense.
2. Lay the tarot card in front of the incense.
3. Hold the image of the person who has wronged you in front of the mirror, so they can see themselves truly.
4. After a few moments, lay the person's image to the left of the tarot card.

5. Lay the image of the scale, which represents balance and justice, to the right of the tarot card.
6. Sprinkle the cedar chips/bark into the fireproof container and light them.
7. Ask Nemesis for her assistance in rectifying the wrong.
8. Drop the images of the person and the scale into the fireproof container.
9. As you watch them burn, feel confident that Nemesis will come to your aid. This act also turns the matter over to her and lets you release animosity or angst.
10. Return the tarot card to the deck.

*"[S]ummer fades and passes, and October comes...
an unsuspected sharpness, a thrill of nervous, swift elation,
a sense of sadness and departure."*

—Thomas Wolfe, American author, *You Can't Go Home Again*

OCTOBER

One of the most beautiful months in the Northern Hemisphere, October dazzles us with its beauty—like the gorgeous goddesses Frigg, Aphrodite, and Hera. However, it's also a harbinger of death. The goddesses Ma'at and Hecate personify this descent into winter's dark time of endings, rest, and reckoning. As you meet the goddesses associated with this time of transition and learn about their experiences, you'll gain insight into transitions you may be going through and how to handle them.

FRIGG

DATES FOR INVITING HER: *October 2–8*

The highest-ranking goddess in Norse mythology, Frigg governs marriage and motherhood, and embodies the fertility, richness, and maturity we associate with the harvest season of life. The harvest is about bringing your gifts and powers to fruition and expressing them fully.

HERSTORY

Frigg's name means "beloved," and this goddess of love and marriage is one of the most revered and powerful deities in the Norse pantheon. She's married to the top god, Odin, and in this capacity serves as queen of the Aesir (one of the two main tribes in Norse mythology). In much the same way the matron of a noble house might run things in the mundane world, Frigg oversees domestic life, handles social arrangements and protocols, entertains dignitaries, and keeps peace in Asgard, the highest realm on the sacred world tree Yggdrasil, which myth says grows at the center of the cosmos.

Legends tell us Frigg has another important job as well. She governs destiny and weaves the future, along with the woolen fabric from which the Aesir's garments are made. As a goddess of fate—known as Wyrd in Norse mythology—naturally she possesses clairvoyance. She alters the course of events on earth by using a type of magic known as *seidr*, symbolically re-weaving threads in her cosmic cloth.

Symbols and Correspondences

We're indebted to Frigg for giving us clouds. According to some legends, she wove them from sheep's wool; others say that the goddess shook out her eiderdown comforter and the feathers formed fluffy white clouds.

Also considered the goddess of motherhood, Frigg embodies the ideal qualities of a good mother: unconditional love, protection, compassion, and nurturance. Women who wanted to become pregnant sought her aid, and mortal mothers looked to her for guidance. Her own story as a mother is a sad one, however. On the longest night of the year, the winter solstice, Frigg gave birth to a beautiful son, Baldur, the god of light and joy. (Here we see similarities to the Christmas story.)

Her other son, Hodor, was blind and known as the god of darkness. The trickster god, Loki, duped Hodor into shooting Baldur with an arrow poisoned by the juice of mistletoe. Devastated, Frigg tried to convince Hel, goddess of the underworld, to let Baldur live—and she agreed, but only if Frigg could get all creatures on earth to grieve her son. Only one, a giant named Thokk, refused, thus sealing Baldur's fate.

Her Animal Totems

Birds of prey were favorites of Frigg, including hawks, falcons, and ravens. Sometimes she's depicted wearing a cloak made of raven feathers. Folklore also tells us the goose was sacred to her.

REASONS TO INVITE HER

In early Germanic cultures, women who wanted children petitioned Frigg—you, too, can seek assistance from this goddess of fertility. As a mother who lost her beloved son, Frigg also offers hope and solace to bereaved women whose children have passed into the afterlife.

As the Norse goddess of matrimony, Frigg can help women who want to attract mates with whom they can form enduring partnerships. If you worry that your partner has commitment issues, ask Frigg's advice for overcoming his or her fears. Unlike fellow Norse goddess Freya (April 17–23), who's considered more of a libertine when it comes to love and sex, myths link Frigg with legalized marriage. She'll also share her secrets for managing domestic affairs, running a household, and entertaining guests. Therefore, Frigg is a patroness of wives married to powerful men and who quietly guide the forces that make patriarchal governance possible.

HOW TO INVITE HER

This activity solicits the aid of Frigg and asks her to bring you a partner who's right for you in every way. You'll need:

- *A ballpoint pen*
- *1 pink candle*
- *1 red candle*
- *Jasmine, rose, or ylang-ylang essential oil*
- *Matches or a lighter*
- *A copper, iron, or earthenware bowl*
- *Cold water*

1. With the ballpoint pen inscribe the letter *X*—the Norse rune for *love*—on the candles.
2. Anoint the candles, which represent you and your partner, with the essential oil (don't rub oil on the wick).

3. Light the candles and drip two small blobs of wax in the bowl. Set the candles in the melted wax to hold them in place.

4. Imagine you and your soul mate together. Feel this person's presence forming in the air around you.

5. Let the candles burn all the way down, so the pink and red wax melt together in the bowl.

6. While the wax is still warm, shape it with your fingers to form a heart, mingling the pink and red.

7. While the wax is still warm, empty the cold water into the bowl so the wax doesn't stick. Remove the wax heart and place it in your bedroom, or if you know feng shui, in the Relationship Gua (when you stand at your front door looking in, this is the far right section of your home).

APHRODITE

DATES FOR INVITING HER: *October 9–15*

In many parts of the Northern Hemisphere, October is one of the loveliest times of the year. This week, therefore, we celebrate the Greek goddess Aphrodite, who personifies love, beauty, art, peace, and pleasure. Her signature fruit, the apple, is in season now too.

> ### Friends and Foes
>
> According to the Greek poet Hesiod, Aphrodite had three companion goddesses known as the Charites: Aglaea, whose name means "splendor"; Euphrosyne, whose name means "good cheer"; and Thalia, whose name means "abundance."

HERSTORY

One of the best-known goddesses in the Greek pantheon, this love goddess was co-opted by the Romans as Venus, and she has equivalents in many cultures worldwide, including Amaterasu (July 17–23) in Japan and Oshun (August 14–20) in West Africa. Aphrodite bears a resemblance to the earlier Sumerian goddess Inanna (April 10–16) and may have derived from her. Although sensuality is one of her main attributes, Aphrodite is also revered for her intellect and knowledge of art, culture, and the finer things in life.

As the goddess of erotic love, Aphrodite had many lovers, including the god Ares. In the *Odyssey*, Homer describes her as being married to the god Hephaestus, and when the sun god Helios discovered her adultery he told Aphrodite's husband. Hephaestus, a metalsmith, made a gold net and trapped Aphrodite and Ares in flagrante delicto. He then embarrassed his wife by inviting the other deities to witness their infidelity. Other myths say the handsome mortal Adonis was one of her consorts.

According to the *Iliad*, Aphrodite took part in a beauty contest in which she competed against two other Olympian goddesses: Hera (October 16–22) and Athena (January 22–28). The Trojan prince Paris was chosen to judge the contest. Poor Paris didn't know what he was getting himself into when he accepted a bribe from Aphrodite—the deal being that if he named her the winner he could have the hand of Helen of Troy, the most desirable woman on the planet. He accepted and awarded Aphrodite the prize: a golden apple. The love goddess kept her part of the bargain, but the resulting affair led to the Trojan War, reminding us to be careful what we wish for.

Her Animal Totems

Art and legend often show Aphrodite with a dove, symbol of peace. Sometimes she's pictured riding in a chariot drawn by doves. The goddess also appears with swans, which represent love, grace, and beauty.

REASONS TO INVITE HER

The winner of perhaps the most elevated beauty contest ever, Aphrodite can show you how to appreciate, accentuate, and express your own beauty. The word *aphrodisiac* comes from her name—this goddess was notorious for inspiring love and lust among the gods as well as mortals. She can guide you in all aspects of the art of romance and love, whether you want to attract a new partner or to increase the passion in your current relationship.

HOW TO INVITE HER

Invite Aphrodite to help you increase the ardor in a romantic relationship by making a flowery love talisman. Note that all the flowers used in this ritual are associated with love and sensuality. You'll need:

- *A pretty bowl, perhaps one decorated with a floral design*
- *Dried red rose petals*
- *Dried apple blossoms*
- *Dried myrtle flowers*
- *Dried jasmine petals*
- *7 love poems—ones by poets you like or ones you've written yourself*
- *A red drawstring pouch (preferably silk)*

1. Set the bowl on a table or other place where it can remain for the week.
2. Fill the bowl with the dried flowers and mix them together with your hands.
3. Call upon Aphrodite and ask her to help you achieve your heart's desire.
4. Read a poem aloud, while you envision enjoying the love you seek. Feel the goddess's energy infusing you with her divine power of attraction.
5. Repeat for another six days.
6. At the end of the seven days, fill the silk pouch with the dried petals and tie it closed with three knots. Thank the goddess for her help. (If you have any of the flower mix left over, sprinkle it outside your home.)
7. Place the talisman on your nightstand or sleep with it under your pillow.

HERA

DATES FOR INVITING HER: *October 16–22*

Like many autumn goddesses, the Greek's Hera represents the fullness of the season, whose dazzling beauty surpasses the budding loveliness of spring's nubile deities. This week we recognize her as a feminine ideal held for millennia, that of wife and mother, and symbol of the institution of marriage.

HERSTORY

Wife of the top Greek god, Zeus, Hera is known as the goddess of marriage and monogamy. Despite her husband's notorious infidelity, she remained loyal to him and didn't engage in extramarital affairs, as did many of her fellow Olympians. Zeus sorely tested his wife's patience with his philandering, and perhaps she can be forgiven for taking out her anger on his lovers and illegitimate offspring.

Hera's vengeance came down hardest on Hercules, Zeus's son with the mortal Alcmene. The goddess tasked the fabled hero with twelve dangerous labors (hoping he'd die in the process), which included killing a lion believed to be indestructible, defeating the hideous snaky monster known as the Hydra, and capturing the vicious three-headed dog Cerberus who guarded Hell's gates. Hera also banished Zeus's lover Leto to the island of

Delos, where she gave birth to his bastard son Apollo. And she turned Callisto into a bear that the hunter goddess Artemis killed.

Her Animal Totems

Peacocks, which represent pride and beauty, are associated with Hera; artists sometimes portray her riding in a chariot drawn by the magnificent birds. According to one story, Hera fashioned the eye-like designs on the peacock's tail from the one hundred eyes of Zeus's murdered son Argos.

In the well-known tale of the Judgment of Paris, Hera took part in a beauty contest with fellow goddesses Aphrodite (October 9–15) and Athena (January 22–28). The contest was rigged, however, and Hera lost to Aphrodite. She got back at Paris for his unfair decision by throwing her lot against his homeland of Troy in the Trojan War and helping to bring about its defeat.

Although mythology paints Hera as a jealous and wrathful goddess, her actions stem from a desire for justice. Only those who had wronged her by betraying the rules of fidelity and honesty suffered her revenge. She offered protection to those who displayed moral character or who helped her, including the hero Jason of the Argonauts.

REASONS TO INVITE HER

Do you feel your spouse or partner doesn't show you the respect you deserve? Is infidelity or jealousy a problem in your relationship? This goddess of marriage can advise you in dealing with an inequitable situation or addressing indiscretions. Ask Hera to lend you her strength and determination when you need to stand up for yourself. She can also help you remain true to a commitment when you're tempted to throw in the towel. If a person has cheated you out of something you deserved or betrayed you for his or her own gain, ask Hera to bring about justice. Female athletes can also solicit help from Hera, in whose honor the Heraean women's sporting events were held, beginning around 800 B.C.E.

HOW TO INVITE HER

Invite Hera to join you in fashioning this gemstone talisman to promote love and fidelity in a primary partnership. You'll need:

- *A piece of pink paper*
- *A pen or marker*
- *2 (3" x 3") squares of dark blue cloth*
- *A piece of rose quartz (for love)*
- *A piece of onyx (for strength and stability)*
- *A piece of sodalite (for harmony and trust)*
- *A piece of chrysoprase (for fidelity and emotional healing)*
- *White thread*
- *A needle*

1. On the paper, write what you seek or want to strengthen in your relationship; for example, "I can trust and rely on my partner at all times and in all situations." Write as many statements as you like, remembering to word them in a positive way.
2. Fold the paper and lay it on one piece of blue cloth.
3. Lay the gemstones on the piece of paper.
4. Place the second piece of blue cloth on top of everything.
5. Thread the needle and sew the two pieces of cloth together. With each stitch, focus on bringing about the intentions you wrote on the paper and on enjoying a happy, fulfilling, committed partnership. Then place it in your bedroom.

MA'AT

During the first week of the sun's ingress into the zodiac sign Scorpio, which astrologers connect with death, transformation, and the afterlife, we recognize the Egyptian goddess Ma'at. This goddess judged humankind posthumously and decided where souls ended up after they left the physical world.

HERSTORY

She who decides whether or not a soul gets into heaven wields tremendous power indeed. For the ancient Egyptians, that power lay in the hands of the goddess Ma'at. When someone died, she placed the person's heart—or soul, by some accounts—on one side of a set of cosmic scales. On the other side, she laid an ostrich feather. If the heart weighed in lighter than the feather, meaning it was free of sin and corruption, Ma'at allowed the soul to enter the afterlife. Otherwise, she tossed it to a lion god named Ammit to eat. No one, not even the pharaohs, escaped the goddess's judgment.

Ma'at's responsibilities extended into other areas of life as well. She embodied truth and kept order in the universe. On earth, she governed the cycle of the seasons. In the skies, she held the celestial bodies in place and guided their orbits. And, like a divine manager, she balanced the relationships between our planet and the heavens. This goddess also presented a code that instructed the Egyptian people in matters of ethical conduct and correct action. Thus Ma'at represents right living, harmony, truth, and justice in this world and in the great beyond.

Symbols and Correspondences

Legends often depict Ma'at with feathers. Not only does she weigh the heart/soul of a deceased person against an ostrich feather to determine its worthiness; artists' images often show her with feathered wings or wearing a single feather in her headdress. The Egyptian hieroglyph for "truth" is a feather.

REASONS TO INVITE HER

This goddess of truth and justice can assist you in any sort of legal matter—she'll shepherd you through the process and help you get fair treatment. Ma'at can come to your aid in other areas where you seek equity too, in your workplace or personal life. If you feel a relationship lacks balance, ask the goddess to intervene and right the situation. If you sense someone isn't being honest with you or that something suspect is going on beneath the surface, let Ma'at show you how to ferret out the truth.

When you need to make an important decision, Ma'at provides insight and enables you to see what's in your best interest. If your life seems chaotic or you want more harmony, Ma'at can help you establish order. This goddess of the afterlife also offers clarity and support to people who have lost loved ones or who may be facing their own deaths.

Friends and Foes

According to mythology, Ma'at had a divine protector, the fierce lion goddess Sekhmet (July 24–30). In ancient Egypt, the term *ma'at* also referred to the system of law and order on earth.

HOW TO INVITE HER

Invite Ma'at into your life by making this good luck talisman that will help swing a decision in your favor when you feel that you may not be judged fairly or that the odds are against you. You'll need:

- *Cinnamon incense*
- *An incense holder*
- *Matches or a lighter*
- *A piece of paper*
- *A pen, pencil, or marker that writes gold ink*
- *3 bay laurel leaves*
- *A white feather*
- *A piece of hematite*
- *A clear quartz crystal*
- *A box large enough to hold these objects but small enough to carry easily*
- *A blue ribbon*

1. Fit the incense into the holder and light it.
2. On the piece of paper, write a request to Ma'at, expressing the outcome you desire. Frame your request in a positive way.
3. Fold the paper three times and place it in the box.
4. Put the bay leaves, feather, hematite, and crystal in the box.
5. Tie the box shut with the blue ribbon, making nine knots. Each time you tie a knot, envision yourself achieving your objective in a way that is just and fair.
6. Let the incense finish burning down and thank the goddess for her assistance.
7. Carry the box with you or set it in a place where you'll see it often.

HECATE

DATES FOR INVITING HER:
October 30–November 5

On October 31, Wiccans and pagans celebrate Samhain, the most sacred sabbat (holy day) of the year. Therefore, we honor the Greek goddess Hecate, the patroness of witches, this week.

Friends and Foes

When Hades abducted Demeter's daughter Persephone and whisked her away to his underground kingdom, Hecate journeyed with the bereaved mother goddess into that dark and frightening realm. Together, Persephone, Demeter, and Hecate represent what's known as the Triple Goddess, three deities who together depict the three stages of a woman's life: maiden, mother, and crone.

HERSTORY

This powerful goddess is known as the queen of the night and goddess of the dark moon, for she rules over the starry sky as well as portions of the earth and the seas. She's also at home in the spirit world. Legends say she keeps company with ghosts and visits graveyards at night. Her familiarity with the realm of the dead made Hecate the logical guide for the goddess

Demeter (September 18–24) when she descended into the underworld to rescue her daughter from the god Hades.

Versed in the magical arts, Hecate knows the secrets of plants for healing and spellwork, and shares her skills with witches. She can see the past, present, and future too, and presides over the art of divination. To people she deems worthy, Hecate grants wishes.

Sometimes called the goddess of the crossroads, Hecate stands at the point where paths converge and where decisions must be made. Here this wise deity offers guidance to those who face conundrums and must choose which direction to take on the road of life. Sometimes she's depicted holding a key that unlocks mysteries or a torch that shines light into murky situations. The ancient Greeks built shrines to her to solicit her protection, and she was known to watch over even the poor and homeless.

Her Animal Totems

Folklore tells us Hecate kept animal companions as familiars, who aided her in her magic work: two dogs, a skunk, and an owl. They not only served practical roles in their animal forms, but were also the embodiments of higher beings: A black female dog was a manifestation of the Trojan queen Hecuba, and the skunk a wise woman cursed by the goddess Eileithyia. The owl symbolized occult knowledge.

REASONS TO INVITE HER

Samhain is a time for remembering those who've left the physical plane, and Hecate, who journeys between the worlds with ease, can help you communicate with your loved ones on the Other Side. She can also make you more aware of the insights and guidance that spirits share with you while you sleep, in the form of dreams.

If you are at a juncture in your life and must make a decision, Hecate, who stands at the crossroads on the path, can put you in touch with your inner knowing so you can choose wisely. This elder goddess doesn't fear what lies ahead, or if she does she's strong enough to handle whatever trials confront her. She'll accompany you if the way seems dark or uncertain, and she'll keep you safe as you travel down your chosen road.

HOW TO INVITE HER

The ancient Greeks honored Hecate at places where roads intersected. In some schools of thought, all paths are related and lead to the Divine. Our thoughts serve as the first steps in generating physical results. This week you can engage the goddess's assistance by enacting an age-old ritual. You'll need:

- *Paper*
- *Pencils, markers, crayons, or paint*
- *Scissors*
- *3 ribbons, each about a foot long*
- *Transparent adhesive tape, glue, or a stapler*
- *A wooden pole*
- *Mushrooms and/or nightshade vegetables*

1. On paper, draw or paint three faces—one represents the past, another the present, and the third the future. Include images, words, and symbols that describe the situation(s) for which you seek Hecate's help.
2. Use the scissors to cut out the faces, then attach the ribbons to them with tape, glue, or staples.
3. Go to a spot where three paths come together, preferably in a rural or secluded spot.
4. Position the pole at the intersection and tie the paper faces to the pole. One looks to the past, one examines the present, and one foresees the future.
5. Leave the veggies at the base of the pole as an offering for the goddess. Thank her and know that your request will be heard.

> *"October extinguished itself in a rush of howling winds and driving rain and November arrived, cold as frozen iron."*
>
> —J.K. Rowling, English author, *Harry Potter and the Order of the Phoenix*

NOVEMBER

At this cold, bleak time we retreat into ourselves, embracing solitude, introspection, self-reliance, fortitude, and the soul-searching that accompanies a period of decline. Now the goddesses of winter—Kali, Nephthys, Rhiannon, and Baba Yaga—guide us through fear into the promise of an afterlife. The deities you'll meet in this section share their stories of dark times and difficulties with you. If you're being tested or you must do battle with an aspect of your life, their experiences can help you confront, with courage and determination, the things that frighten you.

KALI

DATES FOR INVITING HER: *November 6–12*

In India, the festival Kali Puja, where followers gather to worship the Hindu goddess Kali, takes place during October or November on the night of Kartik Amavasya, the new moon day. Folklore says that evil spirits abound on this night, but the fierce destroyer goddess protects her people from harm. This week, we, too, honor Kali and ask her to keep us safe.

Symbols and Correspondences

Art and legends connect Kali with skulls, which represent the cycle of life, death, and rebirth. Of course, the skull also safeguards the body's most important organ: the brain. Use a small likeness of a skull as a symbol of protection or strength.

HERSTORY

Wearing a necklace of skulls and brandishing a bloody sword, Kali is a fearsome sight indeed. Sometimes she wears a skirt made of severed arms and holds a head in one of her four hands. One myth tells us the goddess Durga birthed Kali from her forehead during a time when powerful demons had brought chaos to India, forcing the gods to hide out in the Himalayas. With her two companions, the ferocious Kali made short work of the demons.

She sliced off their heads and hung them around her neck to demonstrate her divine strength and courage.

However, Kali's bloodlust didn't end when she'd finished off the last of the demons—she started indiscriminately slaying everyone who crossed her path. It soon became evident that the goddess had lost control of her reason and must be stopped, so that peace could return to India. The great Lord Shiva, determined to halt Kali's reign of destruction, lay down in front of her. When she accidentally stepped on his chest and realized what she'd done, she stopped fighting.

Kali's struggle against evil involves combating not only outer demons, but inner ones as well. Usually depicted as a dark-skinned goddess with a blood-red tongue, she's a formidable force in a dangerous world. Thus Kali is both feared and loved by her followers, for she keeps devils at bay and brings peace out of chaos.

Friends and Foes

According to legends, Kali is sometimes viewed as an incarnation of the Hindu goddess Durga, or as Durga's daughter, or the destructive aspect of Durga. She's also linked with the Hindu goddess Tara (June 12–18) in her blue and black aspects.

REASONS TO INVITE HER

Are you dealing with people or conditions that wreak havoc in your life? Is an adversary threatening your peace of mind? If so, call upon Kali to help you disperse tension, overcome enemies, and eliminate the causes of distress that are interfering with your well-being. If the demons lie within you in the form of, for example, addictive habits or unhealthy attitudes, Kali can show you how to cut them loose and free yourself from their influence. She'll put you in touch with your innate power and give you the courage to assert yourself with confidence. With her sharp sword, she can slice through illusions and unfounded fears, enabling you to take control of your life.

HOW TO INVITE HER

Kali Puja, which means "Kali worship," has two purposes: to eradicate evil and to bring happiness and peace. The following ritual draws upon traditional elements of her festival. You'll need:

- *Lentils and rice (and spices of your choosing)*
- *Modeling clay*
- *A colorful Indian shawl or tablecloth*
- *1 black and 1 white candle*
- *2 candleholders*
- *Matches or a lighter*
- *Red hibiscus flowers (if you can't find real flowers, use paper ones or pictures downloaded from the Internet)*
- *Firecrackers or sparklers (optional)*

1. Prepare a dish of lentils and rice, adding any other ingredients you choose.
2. While the lentils are cooking, fashion an image of the goddess from the modeling clay.
3. Spread the shawl or tablecloth on your dining table. Then put the candles in the candleholders, place them on the table, and light them.
4. Set the clay image between the candles, and arrange the flowers around her.
5. Invite Kali to join you as you eat the ritual meal of lentils and rice. When you sense her presence, explain to her your situation and ask her to assist you in bringing about the result you desire.
6. After you've finished eating, extinguish the candles. Light sparklers or set off fireworks if you want to (and if it's safe and legal where you live). Otherwise, turn on the lights inside and outside your home to chase away evil spirits. Thank Kali with prayers and mantras.

NEPHTHYS

DATES FOR INVITING HER: *November 13–19*

As the nights grow longer and the earth closes in on herself during this period of decay and death, we honor Nephthys, the Egyptian goddess of death. But just as we know the earth will reawaken again, Nephthys assures us that our souls, too, will be reborn in the afterlife and that death is an illusion.

HERSTORY

Known as the friend of the dead, Nephthys guided the souls of the deceased into the afterlife and protected them in their transition from one realm to another. Not only did she keep the pharaohs safe during their earthly existence; she also guarded them on their journey into the world beyond. When the tomb of King Tutankhamun was discovered in 1922, archaeologists found images of the goddess in it. She presided over funeral rites and gave comfort to the bereaved—ordinary individuals as well as royalty.

The goddess is probably best known in Egyptian mythology for assisting her more famous sister, Isis (July 10–16), after Nephthys's jealous husband, Set, killed Isis's husband (Set's older brother) Osiris, and dismembered him. The two sisters scoured the earth until they managed to collect the pieces of Osiris's body and revive him. According to a 3,000-plus-year-old ritual poem called "The Lamentations of Isis and Nephthys," the goddesses petitioned Osiris to return to the physical world, which had fallen into ruin since his demise.

Where to Seek Her

Nephthys is said to attend funerals and memorial services. You can also sense her presence in cemeteries, where she dispenses peace and solace to those who fear leaving the earthly realm. Here you can receive the wisdom she offers and gain hope concerning your soul's continuity.

Another legend describes Nephthys as a protector deity who makes sure the sun rises every day—another depiction of light and darkness as representations of life and death. According to the story, she stood watch each night to prevent a serpent named Apophis from killing the sun god Ra and destroying the earth. Thus, the goddess serves as both a guardian of life on earth and a guide to the hidden realms beyond.

As a traveler between the realms of the living and the dead, Nephthys also was a keeper of mysteries. Occultists who deal with hidden knowledge and witches of many stripes still look to her as a patroness. Her shamanic powers enable her to traverse the many levels of consciousness and worlds beyond worlds. Symbolically, the goddess is said to possess the power to see in the dark, which makes her privy to knowledge that's ordinarily concealed from the rest of us—even from her fellow deities.

REASONS TO INVITE HER

Have you lost a loved one and wonder whether he or she still lives in some level of being? Are you grieving and long for peace of mind? If so, invite Nephthys to share her knowledge of the world beyond with you. If you fear the inevitable end of earthly existence, ask the goddess to teach you the secrets of life, death, and rebirth. Nephthys can also shine light into hidden areas and offer you power over the darkness that frightens you.

Her Animal Totems

The mythical phoenix that rose from the dead is one of Nephthys's spirit creatures and a symbol of her role as a guide to the afterlife. Legends also put this goddess in the company of hawks and falcons, birds known for their keen eyesight, and artists sometimes show her with feathered wings.

HOW TO INVITE HER

With this ritual, you invite Nephthys to assist you in accepting a loss—whether it be a person, pet, job, home, or something else. Traditionally, prayers are offered to the goddess at night. You'll need:

- *A wooden box*
- *Something that symbolizes your loss*
- *An image of an ankh, the Egyptian symbol of life*
- *Myrrh essential oil*
- *A picture of a phoenix*
- *Dead Sea salt*

1. In the wooden box, which represents a coffin, place the object that symbolizes your loss.
2. Add a representation of an ankh and dot it with myrrh oil.
3. Add a picture of a phoenix, symbol of resurrection.
4. Sprinkle some of the sea salt in the box.
5. Close the box and bury it in a place that signifies renewal to you. Sprinkle more sea salt on the grave.
6. As you put your loss to rest, sense Nephthys's energy easing your suffering, while she simultaneously promises hope for better times ahead.

RHIANNON

DATES FOR INVITING HER: *November 20–26*

The sun is now in Sagittarius, the sign astrologers associate with horses and the half-horse/half-man centaur that is the sign's symbol. Sagittarius is also the sign of travel, both physical and spiritual, so this week we honor the Welsh goddess Rhiannon, a horsewoman of extraordinary skill and speed. She's also a shaman who journeys between the worlds of the living and the dead.

HERSTORY

This beautiful, red-haired goddess hails from a place known as Annwfn (the Otherworld), where Celtic mythology tells us the deities live, or perhaps from the land of the fey, or fairies. Welsh stories written down in the twelfth and thirteenth centuries, known as *The Mabinogion*, describe this goddess as a fairy woman, daughter of the fairy king and the queen of Gwent. Her job was to ride her horse across the sky every day and guide the sun's path from dawn to dusk.

Like all goddesses, feyfolk, and shamans, Rhiannon was a shapeshifter and possessed the ability to travel to many realms of existence. One day while riding her white horse across the wild Welsh terrain she slipped into the physical world where she caught the eye of a mortal—and not just an ordinary guy but Pwyll, the king of Dyfed in southwestern Wales. He tried to catch her, but the swift goddess eluded him until he begged her to marry him and she acquiesced.

> ### Her Animal Totems
> Folklore tells us Rhiannon not only loved horses, but that she was also accompanied by birds wherever she went. Her magical birds' songs had the power to heal people and to bring the dead back to life.

Rhiannon's marriage quickly went downhill. She bore a son to King Pwyll, but mysteriously the child vanished, perhaps kidnapped by one of Rhiannon's earlier and jealous suitors or someone else who wished her harm. When servants framed Rhiannon for killing the baby, Pwyll punished his wife by forcing her to sit outside the city's gate and confess to one and all a crime she didn't commit. She even carried folks who had business with Pwyll on her back, like a horse. Finally, after seven years, the missing boy was discovered in a neighboring stable, where he displayed his mother's equine facility. Rhiannon's unfair ordeal ended, and she was reinstated as queen of Dyfed.

REASONS TO INVITE HER

Stories about Rhiannon suggest she was an intelligent, confident, freedom-loving deity. Nonetheless, she accepted the unfair punishment her husband laid on her and bore the subsequent cruel humiliation with forbearance and dignity. When you feel unjustly judged or burdened, when you're at your wits end and just want to give up, Rhiannon can help you reach into your deepest regions and draw upon the inner reserves of courage, patience, and perseverance you possess to carry on. By stoically sitting with a challenge, instead of running away, you can summon the power to face and overcome it.

HOW TO INVITE HER

This meditation lets you experience the healing nature of birdsong. Spending time in the natural world, communing with wildlife, can ease stress and provide strength and stability. You'll need:

- *Wild birdseed (Birds need extra nutrition during cold weather—find out what birds live in your area at this time of the year and buy what's appropriate, perhaps a mix that contains dried fruit and nuts. Cardinals like sunflower seeds.)*

1. If you live in a rural or suburban area, spend time outdoors listening to the birds in your neighborhood. Or, go to a park.
2. Scatter birdseed on the ground.
3. Turn off your phone so you won't be distracted. Allow your mind to grow quiet.
4. Contemplate a problem you're facing, one in which you feel disrespected, misunderstood, or unfairly treated. Ask Rhiannon to speak to you and offer guidance.
5. Listen to the birdsong around you. What do you intuit the birds are saying? Can you hear Rhiannon's voice among them, sharing her wisdom with you?
6. Pay attention to insights that arise in your mind now—this is the goddess's way of advising and encouraging you as you grapple with your challenge.

7. Feel a sense of peace descending around you as Rhiannon infuses you with her strength and the birds heal you with their music. If you happen to find a feather on the ground, keep it as a token of the goddess's love.

8. Repeat this meditation each day of this week, if possible. Thank the goddess for accompanying you and bolstering your courage.

BABA YAGA

DATES FOR INVITING HER:
November 27–December 3

As the sun continues its descent into darkness, we recognize the Russian goddess Baba Yaga, who appears in folklore and fairy tales as a rather frightening character linked with death. Her home in the deep forest symbolizes the secret place where shamanic wisdom and hidden truths lie, waiting for us to bravely seek them out, as well as the isolation of winter when we metaphorically look within and face our fears of death. This week, we honor her and the annual season of endings, solitude, and decline that precede renewal.

HERSTORY

Like other winter goddesses, Baba Yaga is linked with darkness, decay, and death. And, like many such deities, she's depicted as an old woman. Russian folklore portrays Baba Yaga as a cruel and bloodthirsty hag who lives in the forest and dines on children. According to some stories, she lives in a hut perched on huge chicken legs and surrounded by a fence made of bones and skulls. Baba Yaga uses a unique form of transportation to get around the forest: a mortar and pestle, in which she grinds herbal medicines and the bones of her enemies.

Prior to the advent of Christianity, which demonized many powerful goddesses and female spirits, this frightening deity occupied a position of respect. The mortar and pestle in which she rides identify her as a healer. Her ferocity symbolizes all that is wild and primal in nature. Old myths called her Mother Time and said she knew the secrets of the Other Side. Baltic lore describes her as a wise elder who guards the Waters of Life and Death. Like many winter goddesses, she represents the necessity of death and destruction before rebirth can occur. We see this idea in a Slavic folk belief that a woman who ate the last grain from the harvest, known as the "baba," would give birth when springtime came.

REASONS TO INVITE HER

Baba Yaga shows you how to confront the dark places inside you without flinching. If you're struggling with inner demons, she'll give you courage to stand up to your fears and to rout out obstacles that are interfering with your progress. During times of isolation or loneliness, Baba Yaga teaches the value of solitude in your search for wisdom. If you're experiencing a death, symbolic or physical, she'll guide you through the transition and share with you the secrets of life, death, and rebirth. You can also call upon this fearless and formidable goddess to provide protection in every area of your life.

HOW TO INVITE HER

Call upon Baba Yaga to lend her fierce power to this herbal protection amulet. She'll help keep you and your home safe. You'll need:

- *Dried basil leaves*
- *Dried oregano*
- *Dried rosemary*
- *Fennel seeds*
- *Garlic, fresh or powdered*
- *A mortar and pestle*
- *A black silk, cotton, or leather pouch (optional)*

1. Put the herbs and garlic in the mortar and pestle and grind them into a powdery mix.
2. While you work, state a protection affirmation you've composed to Baba Yaga; for example, "My home is protected by the goddess, and I am safe and sound at all times and in all situations."
3. Envision yourself surrounded by a ball of pure white light, then expand that ball to surround your home.
4. If you wish, you can add the herbal mixture to a soup or stew—but remember to save some for Baba Yaga. As you eat, sense the goddess's energy filling you with strength and courage.
5. Alternately you can fill a black pouch with a teaspoonful or so of the ground herbs that you've reserved. Then hang the pouch on the inside of your front door or sprinkle the protection herbs on your doorstep to keep harm at bay.
6. Finally, offer the remaining herbal mixture to Baba Yaga. Take this to a wooded spot and pour it on the ground, beneath a tree. Thank the goddess for her ongoing protection.

DECEMBER

As the solar year draws to an end at the winter solstice, we retreat into the vast and mysterious realm of our inner lives to reflect and to connect with our inner strength. The goddesses of December—Coatlicue, the Goddess of Guadalupe, the Cailleach, and Spider Woman—represent the wisdom that comes through aging and experiencing life's travails. The stories they share with you in this section provide insight into the ongoing cycle of endings and beginnings. If you feel anxious about the future or uncertain about your place in the world, these wise deities point out that you—and everything else on earth—are part of a divine pattern, a cosmic web that connects us all.

COATLICUE

DATES FOR INVITING HER: *December 4–10*

Like many winter goddesses, Coatlicue is usually portrayed as an old woman who has been there, done that, and grown strong in the process. Aztec mythology considers her a formidable force, involved in both life and death. Therefore, at this time of year, which we associate with endings, we recognize the goddess's destructive nature as being essential to the ongoing cycle that leads to renewal.

HERSTORY

The Aztecs honored Coatlicue as a divine matriarch. Like a matriarch of a human clan, she's not only the creative source of everything around her— myth says she birthed the celestial bodies as well as human beings—she also manages our ongoing existence. Nothing in heaven or earth occurs without her putting her stamp on it. She governs everything from birth to death and is a goddess of childbirth and of war, one who directs the fertile planting season and the final harvest.

Coatlicue's name means "serpent skirt," and artists depict her wearing a skirt made of entwined snakes. A statue of the goddess in Mexico City's National Museum of Anthropology shows her with snakes where her head should be, a snake belt with a skull buckle, and claws on her hands and feet. Snakes, of course, signify death and rebirth by shedding their skins, so they present an apt symbol for this goddess.

According to one myth, Coatlicue was busy cleaning a shrine on Snake Mountain when feathers fell from the sky and magically caused her to become pregnant. She was already the mother of the moon goddess Coyolxauhqui and four hundred more children—the stars, known as the Huiztnaua. This immaculately conceived child turned out to be the sun god Huitzilopochtli. Before long a family feud erupted, during which Huitzilopochtli killed his sister and his star-siblings with a solar ray. The story may describe a shift from a matriarchal society to a patriarchal one, as it was written down in the *Florentine Codex* in the late sixteenth century, after the Spanish conquest.

Another legend says that four suns existed before the present one. When it became time for a fifth sun to emerge, a group of goddesses that may have included Coatlicue sacrificed themselves so that life on earth could continue under the new luminary.

Friends and Foes

Folklore connects Coatlicue with a group of dangerous star-deities called the tzitzimime who came to earth for five days each year and terrorized the Aztec people. However, these deities also served as divine midwives who guided mothers and infants through childbirth, continuing the idea of destruction and renewal in Coatlicue's story.

REASONS TO INVITE HER

Because Coatlicue is both a creator and a destroyer, she can assist you when you want to start something new or bring something to a satisfactory conclusion. As the goddess of rejuvenation, she encourages renewed well-being after a period of decline or loss. As a mother deity and divine midwife, she offers protection to women and their newborns. Her terrifying appearance, it's said, scares away harmful entities that might endanger mother or child. If you're birthing another type of creative venture, such as beginning a new job, Coatlicue will lend you her formidable vitality and help you succeed. This cosmic manager can also guide you in the day-to-day operation of a business, family, or collective endeavor. She'll show you how to plant seeds for the future, nurture your crop through the development stages, and reap a rewarding harvest.

> ### Where to Seek Her
> Go outside on a crisp, clear night and gaze up at the stars. According to Aztec folklore, these are Coatlicue's children. Legends tell us we are all her children too. Sense your connection to the goddess; feel her protecting and nurturing you in all you do.

HOW TO INVITE HER

Snakes show up in the myths of many cultures, as symbols of knowledge and power, sexuality and fertility, life, death, and rebirth. This meditation lets you connect with the serpent power of Coatlicue to aid rejuvenation. If possible, acquire a serpentine stone to hold during this meditation on the chakras, the body's vital energy centers.

1. Sit in a place where you feel safe and comfortable, and know you won't be disturbed for a while. Silence your phone, TV, and other distractions.
2. Begin breathing slowly and deeply. Focus on each inhalation and each exhalation, letting your mind grow calm.
3. Envision a ball of glowing red light at the base of your spine, where a school of yoga called kundalini says serpent power resides. Sense the "serpent" that lies here uncoil and begin to twine slowly up your spine.

4. As the serpent rises through your body, feel the power and energy of the serpent awaken, gently removing blocks to your well-being.

5. Allow the energy to pleasantly travel upward in a spiraling motion, enlivening each chakra.

6. When the energy reaches the top of your head, envision it spouting like a beautiful geyser from your crown chakra. Sense it wash down over you, healing and cleansing you in body, mind, and spirit.

7. Sit in meditation as long as you like, then gradually ease back into your everyday awareness. Thank Coatlicue for lending you her power.

GODDESS OF GUADALUPE

DATES FOR INVITING HER: *December 11–17*

This week we honor the Goddess of Guadalupe. In Mexico, the goddess's festival is celebrated on December 12, the day in 1531 when she is said to have appeared in a divine visitation in a location north of Mexico City. On this joyous holiday, revelers thank the goddess for her protection and for providing abundance throughout the year.

HERSTORY

Also known as Our Lady of Guadalupe, this goddess of love, mercy, and compassion is a face of the Virgin Mary, revered in Mexico and other parts of Latin America—but she bears a strong resemblance to the Nahua/Aztec goddess Tonantzin. Mythology tells us this goddess appeared to a Nahua/Aztec man named Juan Diego on the Hill of Tepeyac, a location sacred to the Nahua people. For centuries they had worshipped the earth goddess Tonantzin, whose name means "sacred mother," at a temple there—before the Spanish invaded and tore it down in 1520. The goddess didn't want the native people to forget her and asked Diego to build a place where they could pay their respects.

According to folklore, the goddess told Diego to convey the story of her visitation to the bishop, which he did. The bishop, however, didn't believe him and demanded proof. So the goddess directed Diego to collect rare Castilian roses from the hill—although these roses aren't native to Mexico—and give them to the bishop. He carried the flowers in his tilma (poncho), and when he opened the tilma the bishop saw an image of the goddess imprinted on the cloth and was convinced.

The Goddess of Guadalupe, like Tonantzin before her, is a mother deity who nurtures and protects her people. To Mexicans, she's both a religious and cultural icon. Often the goddess is depicted surrounded by the sun's golden rays. Her shrine, the Basilica of Our Lady of Guadalupe in Mexico City, is one of the most popular sacred sites in the world, visited by millions of people each year.

REASONS TO INVITE HER

Are there areas in your life that could benefit from nurturing, kindness, or compassion? Do you seek validation and understanding, someone to encourage you and let you know you matter? The Goddess of Guadalupe will come to your aid with her generous and boundless love and support you in your endeavors. She'll also teach you to respect yourself and to honor the deities who watch over you.

This benevolent mother goddess can safeguard you and your loved ones in the coming year—you only need ask for her protection. As you mark her holiday this week, focus on the things for which you are grateful—family, friends, good health, work you enjoy, peace, and safety. Let the goddess teach you how to increase your blessings by expressing gratitude for the gifts you've already received.

HOW TO INVITE HER

In Mexico, the goddess's festival includes feasting, music, and dancing. On December 12, invite her and her powers into your life by preparing a ritual meal of traditional Mexican food. Welcome friends and family into your home to share it with you. You can serve dishes such as:

- *Tacos*
- *Chicken mole*
- *Black beans*
- *Rice*
- *Guacamole*
- *Flan*

1. Cover the dining table with a colorful, embroidered cloth and set a vase of red Castilian roses at the center. Display an image of the goddess on the table too.
2. Wear a flowered Mexican shawl and pin a rose in your hair.
3. Toast the goddess with tequila (or fruit juice if you choose not to drink alcohol) and give thanks for the blessings in your life.
4. Throughout the week, play mariachi and traditional Mexican music.
5. Each night light red and gold candles in the Goddess of Guadalupe's honor, or attach her picture to a large pillar candle and dedicate it to the goddess.

THE CAILLEACH

DATES FOR INVITING HER: *December 18–24*

During this week, when we enter the darkest time of the year—the winter solstice—we honor the Celtic winter goddess, the Cailleach, whose name means "veiled one" or "old woman." She presides over this cold, dark, barren time of year and has many faces and variations in the folklore of Ireland, Scotland, and England.

HERSTORY

Often depicted as ugly, wizened, and gloomy, the Cailleach personifies deep winter. In Scotland, she's shown with a blue face, suggesting the bitter weather has turned her blue with cold. Sometimes she's pictured with hair white as snow, carrying a hammer with which she breaks up ice that blocks her way. On the Isle of Man, she's considered a spell-weaver and diviner. Sometimes she's viewed as an ancestral deity; often she's linked with the end stage of life.

According to one myth, the ancient goddess imprisons a young, beautiful goddess within a mountain during the winter season. When the Cailleach sets the youthful deity free, spring emerges from within the earth's dark recesses and the land blossoms once again. Here we see parallels to the story of the Greek goddess Persephone, whom Hades captures and holds in his underground realm during the winter months. It also bears similarities to the Sumerian myth of Inanna (April 10–16), whose descent into the underworld throws the earth into a period of death and decay. Another legend says the Cailleach starts out as an old woman and evolves into a lovely maiden over time, just as winter changes into spring.

Friends and Foes

Myths sometimes speak of a partnership between the Cailleach and another powerful Celtic goddess, Brigid (January 29–February 4). The Cailleach presides over the darkest months, and Brigid has dominion as the days lengthen. In some tellings, the two goddesses are actually two faces of the same deity.

Like other winter goddesses, the Cailleach is a wise woman archetype with magical powers. Scottish folklore credits her with creating the mountains in the Highlands. Numerous sites bear her name, including the mountain Beinn na Caillich on the Isle of Skye and Slieve na Calliagh in Ireland, a hilly passage tomb aligned so that the sun shines into it on the equinoxes. She's also believed to raise ferocious storms, slamming the countryside with sleet and snow, and the howling of the north wind is said to be her voice.

REASONS TO INVITE HER

This ancient goddess, revered for thousands of years, can help you appreciate the wisdom and strength that come with age. If you're in the winter of your life, she can support you through challenges involving loss, decline, or limitations. If you're young, the Cailleach can teach you to value each stage of your journey and to attune yourself with the ongoing cycle of life, death, and rebirth. If you've suffered hardship or feel despairing during a dark time, the Cailleach promises brighter times lie ahead.

HOW TO INVITE HER

Legends tell us that at the end of winter the Cailleach transformed herself into a stone boulder, withdrawing into stillness and silence during the warm months. One tale says the goddess and her family stayed for a while at Tigh nan Cailleach in Perthshire, Scotland, and gifted the people there with magic stones that provided protection. This week, invite the goddess into your life with the power of stones the way those at Tigh nan Cailleach did.

1. This week collect several blue-gray stones that speak to you—these represent the goddess in her many aspects. Stones hold ancient wisdom and memories of the events they've witnessed.

2. Spend some time each day with the stones, allowing them to reveal their secrets to you. If you like, you can form a circle with the stones and sit or stand within it.

3. At the end of the week, position the stones at the front and back of your home to safeguard it. Depending on how many stones you've collected, you might even choose to encircle your home with them.

4. If you wish, give stones to friends or loved ones to protect them as well.

SPIDER WOMAN

DATES FOR INVITING HER: *December 25–31*

As the year draws to a close, we honor the Native American goddess/grandmother Spider Woman, whose divine web holds the world together. In this final week, when the Northern Hemisphere is immersed in death and decay and dark times, she reminds us that we are united with everything in an infinite universe. Nothing exists in isolation and all endings lead to renewal.

Her Animal Totems

The spider signifies the great mother—legend says the goddess has a holy name but it cannot be spoken, so she's called Spider Woman or Spider Grandmother out of respect. If the spider is your totem, you possess creativity and ingenuity, as well as the industriousness to bring your dreams to fruition.

HERSTORY

Many legends about Spider Woman exist among the indigenous tribes of the southwestern United States. They tell us that this creator goddess brought the universe into being with her thoughts, and she continues to manage everything that transpires in the heavens and on earth. Her great web holds together humankind; the animals and birds; plants, rivers, and deserts; as well as the sun, moon, planets, and stars, connecting them to each other in a matrix of consciousness.

One myth tells us Spider Woman created the cosmos by weaving and singing. She fashioned the land and sea from turquoise, red and yellow rocks, and quartz. Another story says the goddess originally had dominion over the underworld region of the deities, whereas the sky god Tawa governed the heavens. Together they formed the earth and populated it with the creatures that now live on our planet. According to another legend, Spider Woman spun a tubular channel that stretched from heaven down to the Grand Canyon, like a divine birth canal, and sent souls through it to incarnate on earth.

This wise teacher schooled humans in the arts of weaving, basketry, and pottery making. Folklore tells us she brought corn to her people and taught them agriculture. She also gave them fire.

Symbols and Correspondences

This divine weaver naturally has fondness for textiles, especially blankets and rugs with bold geometric shapes and bright colors. Colors have numerous symbolic meanings. The Navajo, for example, connect yellow with the west, black with the north, white with the east, and blue with the south.

REASONS TO INVITE HER

Often we feel a lack of genuine connection to the people around us. We long for a sense of community, to belong, and to be able to communicate well with our families, friends, and neighbors. Spider Woman can show you how to live and work harmoniously with others. According to one legend, the goddess taught a lonely girl to spin and weave, and instructed her to share the skill with the women in her tribe. Through teaching them, the girl gained respect and friendship.

Spider Woman also lets you appreciate your connection with all things, not only on this planet but in the spirit world as well. She'll help you learn to listen to the messages conveyed to you by your ancestors, guides, and guardians. If you want to discover more about your biological ancestors, ask Spider Woman to accompany you on your journey into the past.

HOW TO INVITE HER

This week invite the goddess to share insights into how to handle relationships with other people via your dreams. You'll need:

- *A dreamcatcher, which resembles a spider's web*
- *A smudge stick, usually made of sage*
- *Matches or a lighter*
- *A journal or notebook*
- *A pen or pencil*

1. Hang the dreamcatcher above your bed.
2. In the evening, light the smudge stick with your matches or lighter and carry it in a circle around your bedroom, letting its purifying smoke waft through the room and cleanse it of unwanted or inharmonious energies. (Make sure to extinguish the smudge stick before going to sleep.)
3. Place the journal and pen/pencil on your nightstand, so they're handy if you wake during the night and want to jot down a dream.
4. Before falling asleep, set the intention that you will remember and understand your dreams. Ask Spider Woman to speak to you while you sleep.

5. In the morning, as soon as you wake up, write down as much as you can remember about your dreams. Pay attention to the mood of each dream, as well as the people in it and the action that occurs. Note symbols, especially those that recur frequently such as water, cars, houses, animals, etc.

6. Repeat each day of the week. You may want to read some books about dream interpretation or discuss your dreams with other people, but your own impressions are most important.

US/METRIC CONVERSION CHART

VOLUME CONVERSIONS

US Volume Measure	Metric Equivalent
⅛ teaspoon	0.5 milliliter
¼ teaspoon	1 milliliter
½ teaspoon	2 milliliters
1 teaspoon	5 milliliters
½ tablespoon	7 milliliters
1 tablespoon (3 teaspoons)	15 milliliters
2 tablespoons (1 fluid ounce)	30 milliliters
¼ cup (4 tablespoons)	60 milliliters
⅓ cup	90 milliliters
½ cup (4 fluid ounces)	125 milliliters
⅔ cup	160 milliliters
¾ cup (6 fluid ounces)	180 milliliters
1 cup (16 tablespoons)	250 milliliters
1 pint (2 cups)	500 milliliters
1 quart (4 cups)	1 liter (about)

WEIGHT CONVERSIONS

US Weight Measure	Metric Equivalent
½ ounce	15 grams
1 ounce	30 grams
2 ounces	60 grams
3 ounces	85 grams
¼ pound (4 ounces)	115 grams
½ pound (8 ounces)	225 grams
¾ pound (12 ounces)	340 grams
1 pound (16 ounces)	454 grams

OVEN TEMPERATURE CONVERSIONS

Degrees Fahrenheit	Degrees Celsius
200 degrees F	95 degrees C
250 degrees F	120 degrees C
275 degrees F	135 degrees C
300 degrees F	150 degrees C
325 degrees F	160 degrees C
350 degrees F	180 degrees C
375 degrees F	190 degrees C
400 degrees F	205 degrees C
425 degrees F	220 degrees C
450 degrees F	230 degrees C

BAKING PAN SIZES

American	Metric
8 x 1½ inch round baking pan	20 x 4 cm cake tin
9 x 1½ inch round baking pan	23 x 3.5 cm cake tin
11 x 7 x 1½ inch baking pan	28 x 18 x 4 cm baking tin
13 x 9 x 2 inch baking pan	30 x 20 x 5 cm baking tin
2 quart rectangular baking dish	30 x 20 x 3 cm baking tin
15 x 10 x 2 inch baking pan	30 x 25 x 2 cm baking tin (Swiss roll tin)
9 inch pie plate	22 x 4 or 23 x 4 cm pie plate
7 or 8 inch springform pan	18 or 20 cm springform or loose bottom cake tin
9 x 5 x 3 inch loaf pan	23 x 13 x 7 cm or 2 lb narrow loaf or pate tin
1½ quart casserole	1.5 liter casserole
2 quart casserole	2 liter casserole

INDEX

ABOUT THE AUTHOR

Skye Alexander is the author of more than forty fiction and nonfiction books, including *Find Your Goddess: How to Manifest the Power and Wisdom of the Ancient Goddesses in Your Everyday Life*. Her stories have appeared in numerous anthologies internationally, and her books have been translated into more than a dozen languages. She is also an artist, tarot reader, and feng shui practitioner. Visit her website and blogs at SkyeAlexander.com.